CARDINAL NEWMAN'S SCHOOL

150 YEARS OF THE ORATORY SCHOOL, READING

CARDINAL NEWMAN'S SCHOOL

150 YEARS OF THE ORATORY SCHOOL, READING

TONY TINKEL

THIRD MILLENNIUM
PUBLISHING, LONDON

For Meg

1.3.1946 – 1.3.1983

Much loved – much missed

Cardinal Newman's School: 150 years of The Oratory School, Reading
© The Oratory School and Third Millennium Publishing Limited

First published in 2009 by Third Millennium Publishing Limited, a subsidiary of Third Millennium Information Limited.

2–5 Benjamin Street, London United Kingdom EC1M 5QL
www.tmiltd.com

ISBN: 978 1 906507 09 1

British Library Cataloguing in Publication Data
A CIP catalogue record for this book is available from the British Library.

Edited by Susan Millership
Designed by Matthew Wilson
Production by Bonnie Murray
Reprographics by Studio Fasoli, Italy
Printed in Slovenia by Gorenjski-tisk

CONTENTS

AUTHOR ACKNOWLEDGEMENTS

I am grateful to a wide range of people and institutions, who have opened their doors to me and given me great encouragement in the writing of this record of the story of The Oratory School.

I am indebted to the Fathers of the Birmingham Oratory, in particular to the Provost, the Very Reverend Father Paul Chavasse, and to Father Gregory Winterton. Brother Frank McGrath, the Editor of Newman's Letters & Diaries, has been a regular source of help and information. It has been a delight to research in the Archives of the Duke of Norfolk at Arundel Castle and its staff, especially Mrs Rodger, have been ever willing to assist me in my endeavours.

I thank the Governors of the Oratory School Association, under the Chairmanship of Mr Michael Hasslacher, for their constant support and discreet encouragement. To them I am grateful for permission to consult and to quote from the minutes of past deliberations of the Governing Body. My story would have been infinitely the poorer without the support of Mr Anthony Cornwell, who has, without restriction, generously passed on the fruits of his own research into the past of Cardinal Newman's school. He has also given

me the reassurance of impartial advice on draft chapters, stemming from his wide experience of the topic and his considered perspective of the issues involved. He has been the trusted and critical friend that every author requires. So much of the knowledge of the School's past that is to be admired in this work, stems in the first instance from him.

There is a wide range of people to whom I owe much for their contribution to this work. These include the Governors, present and former colleagues, Old Boys and well-wishers, who have been prepared to read draft chapters and comment upon them. Mention must be given in the first instance to the Head Master, Mr Clive Dytor, as well as to his predecessors, Mr Adrian Snow and Mr Maurice Lynn. They have all offered their support and enthusiasm to this project and provided encouragement and input at crucial moments. I am also grateful to Mrs Brenda Barrow for taking the trouble to consider the references in the text to her late husband, Simon. Amongst the members of the Governing Body, all have been ever-ready to tender advice and encouragement on draft chapters and I wish to express my thanks to them for that.

Dora and Andrew Nash head a long list of colleagues and former colleagues whose comments on draft chapters have contributed signally to my morale at difficult moments and have enhanced the worth of what has been produced. The list of such contributors must include Mr Peter Burr, Professor Tony Mallet, Mr Tom McIntyre, Mr Ian McLean, Mrs Linda Coupland, Ms Dawn Chamarette and Monsignor Antony Conlon. This account of helpers and encouragers would not be complete without mention of a number of Old Oratorians, Professor Dominic Baker-Smith, Mr Michael Chapman, the late Sir Michael Levey, the Right Reverend Monsignor Vaughan Morgan, C.B.E., Mr Jim Phillips, Mr Bob Symington, the late Mr Francis Thorneycroft and Dr Henry Will. I would also feel it remiss of me, if I did not thank, as important contributors in this enterprise, Ms Joanna Tolkien, Professor Christopher Brooke and Professor Alan McClelland.

I must also acknowledge the contribution to this work by the O.P.S. for their Chapter on the history of that school. It has helped to give a rounded perspective of the two schools of the Association. I am grateful also to the Head Master, Mr Clive Dytor, for his signal assistance in recasting the final Chapter which tries to look ahead from the vicissitudes of the past.

I wish to offer my particular thanks to Mr Maurice French for permission to quote from his work on his family history, *The Frenchs of French Park*, and to Mr Robin Allott for his permission to quote from his schoolboy letters to his parents. These letters were the vital source of evidence that Lord FitzAlan used his contacts in 1941 to prevent the Army from taking over Woodcote House. I also offer similar thanks to Dr Henry Will, who provided me with invaluable details and help in recounting the story of the dispute between the Fathers of the Birmingham Oratory and the Association over the proceeds of the sale of Caversham Park, as well as to Captain Edward Pereira, the great-nephew of Father Edward Pereira, for his unfailing interest in my opus, in particular for permission to publish letters from his grandmother to his grandfather about the state of health of E.P. during the First World War. I am equally grateful to Dr Paul Shrimpton and his publishers, Gracewing, for permission to use parts of his work on the early days of the School – *A Catholic Eton? Newman's Oratory School*. His encouragement and interest in this project have exceeded the level that I had a right to expect.

Marjorie Trusted, Senior Curator of the Sculpture Department of the Victoria and Albert Museum, and Ms Christine Wallace of the Portmeirian Foundation, have both been most helpful over details, recalling my research enquiry on their resources long after conventional politeness would make it necessary. Mrs Diana Bailey has provided vital information on the renting and later sale to the Oratory Fathers by her great-grandfather, of the playing fields at Ravenhurst in 1873 and 1892.

This book has been an attempt to depict the unfolding story of the life of one of the only two institutions founded by John Henry Cardinal Newman, which still survive to the present day. It is a story of the survival of an educational vision against the odds, which include three changes of location and two financial crises. Nevertheless through all its vicissitudes Newman's educational vision for boys, inspired by St Philip Neri's apostolate among the youth of 16th century Rome, has persisted, adapting to changing times, as the Founder would have expected.

Those who know the School well, see in it the organically evolving substitute for the treatise on secondary education which John Henry Newman never wrote. It has been an honour and a privilege to be commissioned by the Governors of his School to write its history to mark the 150th anniversary of its foundation.

Tony Tinkel
July 2009

FOREWORD

LORD CHIEF JUSTICE OF ENGLAND AND WALES

The Oratory School is celebrating its 150th anniversary this year and I am delighted that we are commemorating the founding of the school by one of England's greatest Victorians – John Henry Cardinal Newman – with the publication of a superbly-illustrated book accompanied by an excellent narrative.

Cardinal Newman's School charts the colourful, compelling and occasionally tempestuous voyage of Newman's venture, from the early days in Birmingham to the Thames Valley where the School flourishes today. As Newman stands on the edge of Beatification,

England's first since the martyrdoms of the 16th century, the book gives insights into his thinking on education and pastoral care and underscores his spiritual influence on the School's past and future.

I am sure you will find the writer, Tony Tinkel, rekindles fond memories of the School, exploring its unique history and traditions. The book also looks ahead, providing both senior and prep school pupils, alumni, their families and staff with an objective but affectionate insight into the ethos and achievements of The Oratory School.

The Right Honourable Lord Judge
Lord Chief Justice of England and Wales
President of the Oratory School Association
July 2009

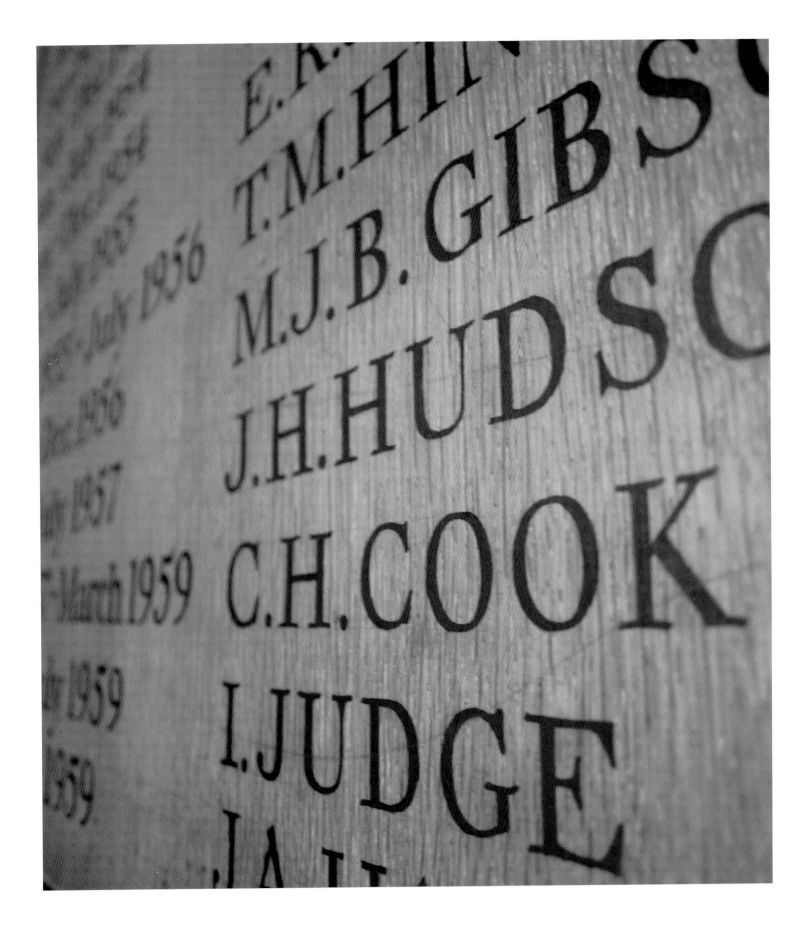

CHAPTER ONE

THE BEGINNINGS

The School's founder, John Henry Newman and the early years in Birmingham, 1858–62

"From first to last, education, in this large sense of the word, has been my line."

– Cardinal Newman

Opposite: John Henry Newman drawn by George Richmond.

Below: John Henry Newman started his undergraduate studies at Trinity College, Oxford in 1817.

There are few schools in Britain that can claim to have a Founder who, monarchs apart, is more famous than the institution itself. The Oratory School can argue validly to be one such school. John Henry Cardinal Newman was respected by his contemporaries and is admired today by scholars and theologians. Pope Benedict XVI, as Cardinal Joseph Ratzinger, hailed Newman as "the greatest of English theologians". This important English figure was responsible for the foundation and the moulding of The Oratory School.

John Henry Newman was born on 21st February, 1801 in the City of London. His father was a banker and his mother, Jemima Fourdrinier, was of French Huguenot descent. In 1808 he was sent to a boarding school at Ealing. Newman's biographer Meriol Trevor gives this appraisal of the early Newman: "[He] had … all the physical and mental equipment of a poet … At the same time he had a mind capable of the clearest abstract reasoning, logical and mathematical."

Newman entered Trinity College, Oxford, in 1817 and was elected a fellow of Oriel College in 1822, where he became a tutor four years later. In 1825 he was ordained to the Anglican priesthood and appointed Vicar of the University Church of St. Mary the Virgin, Oxford where his sermons became famous. He began writing *Tracts for the Times* in 1833. The Oxford Movement, that aimed to revive Catholic doctrine and observance in the Church of England, took its inspiration from these tracts. The tracts grew out of Newman's thinking on spiritual and religious questions. In Tract Number 90 he attempted to interpret the 39 Articles of the Church of England in a sense that was sympathetic to Catholicism which aroused controversy

Left: Newman was received into the Catholic Church by Blessed Dominic Barberi in 1845. Shown here is a detail from a stained glass window at Our Lady of the Passion Monastery, at Daventry commemorating Father Barberi's life.

Below: Newman and Ambrose St John during their time at the seminary in Rome, painted by Maria Giberne.

and marked an important point on his personal spiritual journey. The tract produced public censure from University and Anglican Church figures. He withdrew to Littlemore, a parish on the outskirts of Oxford under the patronage of Oriel College. Earlier he had leased some cottages in the village which were to form the base for a community of his friends. At this stage he was preoccupied with the relationship between Catholicism and the Anglican Church.

In October, 1845 he was received into the Catholic Church at Littlemore by the Italian Passionist priest, Blessed Dominic Barberi. Later that month he went to Oscott College, a seminary near Birmingham, to be confirmed and to see its President Nicholas Wiseman. Wiseman offered Newman and his Oxford converts the use of the old Oscott College building two miles from the new College. Newman later renamed it Maryvale.

In 1846 he went to Rome with his great friend Ambrose St John, who had also been received into the Catholic Church. There they entered the College of Propaganda, a seminary for students from mission countries. Newman was ordained in May, 1847 and embarked on an Oratorian novitiate. An Oratory house would allow Newman to keep his companions with him and had echoes of the Oxford collegiate system. Both of these were important for Newman. He returned to England at the end of 1847 with a papal brief which instructed him to set up a house of the Congregation of the Oratory in Birmingham. This was originally located in a former gin distillery in Alcester Street from where, in 1852, it transferred to the present purpose-built premises in Hagley Road, Edgbaston. From this house, his home until his death in 1890, his national and international influence and prestige emanated.

Earlier, Newman's followers had been joined by those who had settled at Cotton Hall, Staffordshire, under the leadership of Father Frederick Faber. Faber was a former Fellow of University College, Oxford who had become a

Below: The School retains its close relationship with the Birmingham Oratory and in February 2009 it took part in Solemn Vespers there to celebrate the 208th anniversary of Cardinal Newman's birth.

Catholic, and whose colourful personality and devotionalism had attracted a group of converts around him. He had wished to bring his group to join Newman and his friends, but despite appreciating Faber's charisma, Newman realised that they were not meant to work together. The resultant community was split into two, one group remaining in Birmingham with Newman as the Father Superior and the other establishing the London Oratory under the leadership of Father Faber. The latter house was opened in 1849 near the Strand. It was to settle eventually on its present site in South Kensington next to the Brompton Road.

In 1850 a Catholic hierarchy was re-established in England and Wales which led to an outburst of anti-Catholic feeling in the country.

In 1854, a proposal came to Newman that was to fire his imagination and focus his thoughts on education in the Catholic context. He was invited to become the Rector of a proposed Catholic University of Ireland, based in Dublin. He drafted his ideas for the running of this institution in the form of a series of lectures, which now bear the title *The Idea of a University*. This work is regarded as a classic of educational thought. The University was officially opened in November, 1854, but after years of difficulties he tendered his resignation as Rector in November, 1858. This educational scheme was now to be replaced in his life by another – The Oratory School. Newman's efforts in Dublin were not in vain as the University was later to become the basis for the National University of Ireland, Dublin.

Events leading up to the foundation of the School had already been in train during 1858. In that year moves were made by a group of Catholic, mainly convert, laymen to approach Newman as a potential overseer of a Catholic boarding school for boys, run on public school lines.

The Catholic world of 19th-century England was composed of three main groups. Firstly there were the Old Catholics from recusant families, so called as they had refused to conform to the Church of England and had retained their allegiance to Rome throughout the centuries of persecution. They had survived by avoiding attention, which might have led in earlier days, to imprisonment or possibly martyrdom. It could also lead to fines and the confiscation of estates. Secondly, there were the immigrant Irish, who by 1851 had increased to around half a million. Thirdly there were converts, mainly from the Oxford Movement, who were from Anglican professional and clerical middle class backgrounds.

The Old Catholics had been forbidden by the law to give their children a Catholic education in England. So, to offer them the education they wanted for their children, schools were founded on the Continent, attached to and run by houses of religious communities. Catholic parents in England, at some risk to themselves, sent their children to these schools. During the French Revolution and its subsequent wars, these communities were forced to flee to England, where many of the

Now we have got the right Tool and we shall soon get possession of all our Own Churches again

I am as unalterable as my late Brother, even as my lamented Father against any further Power to the Catholics

ABRITISH battering-Ram preparing the way for a POPISH Bull

French émigré clergy had sought refuge. There had been a softening of the anti-Catholic climate in the country and they were able to find safety in their homeland. The laws of restriction on Catholics had been relaxed during the latter part of the 18th century and in 1829, when the Catholic Emancipation Act removed many of the curbs under which the Catholic community of England had suffered since Tudor times.

The 19th-century converts to Catholicism comprised a number of confident, articulate, public school professional men. They were not attracted to the education available for their sons in the Catholic faith in England. So some members of this number decided to approach the most prominent convert to Catholicism of the age, Newman, to help in establishing a school for the Catholic education of their sons which would be more in harmony with the traditional English public school. Many of these men were personal friends of Newman from his days at Oxford.

One influential figure in this approach was Edward Bellasis, Serjeant-in-Law at the House of Lords, who wrote to Newman: "to ask of you, whether, if you were furnished with such funds as would be necessary … you would undertake to start such a school and to nurse it into maturity".

Newman replied swiftly to Bellasis in encouraging terms and with detailed ideas for the accommodation and financial arrangements. Following this exchange of letters, influential members of the convert group went to Birmingham to discuss the project with Newman, Father Ambrose St John and Father Nicholas Darnell. Newman "expressed his sense of the desirability of its object and his readiness to co-operate in its accomplishment".

Bellasis was joined in his efforts by James Hope-Scott, QC. Another key figure associated with the group was Sir John Acton who belonged to a family of Shropshire Catholic gentry and therefore linked the converts and the Old Catholics. He had been born in Naples and his European connections and liberal outlook meant Acton was keen to address what he regarded as the inward-looking frame of mind of much of the 19th-century English Catholic world.

In April, 1858 there was a "Decree of the General Congregation at Edgbaston, giving its sanction to Father Nicholas Darnell being Father Superior's representative in undertaking, at the instance of friends in London, the establishment and formation of a school for lay boys of the upper classes".

Above: A contemporary cartoon illustrating the furore that surrounded the passing of the Catholic Emancipation Act in 1829.

By the end of 1858 one of the promoters could write: "The school plan is fast advancing to maturity, and I think there is every probability that a commencement will really be made at Easter [1859]." The project ran into difficulties from the outset. It fell foul of the tussle between, on the one hand, some of the Old Catholic peers and gentry as well as some converts, who were looking for a more English emphasis to their faith, and those who opposed this. The suspicions that had arisen from that tussle were to cast a shadow over Newman and his school up until his elevation to the cardinalate in 1879, when he commented in hope "the cloud is lifted from me forever".

Promoters of the new school had an impressive list of supporters, including the Duke of Norfolk, Viscount Camden, Lord Feilding and Lord Charles Thynne. Despite the wealth of such figures, measures were not drawn up to ensure the financial stability of the proposed school. Throughout the 19th century, the project was bedevilled by financial worries and needed the generosity of benefactors to survive. Newman's trusting nature allowed a situation to develop where his authority over the new foundation was not clearly defined, and this led directly to the School's first crisis within two years of its beginning.

Newman sent at the end of 1858 a draft manifesto to Bellasis and Hope-Scott, who recast Newman's ideas to identify key points about the proposed project. In February, 1859 the following notice was circulated outlining the agreed points:

"It is the intention of Father Newman, of the Birmingham Oratory, with blessing of God, to commence on 1st May next [date inserted by hand] a School for the education of boys, not destined to the ecclesiastical state, and not above twelve years of age on their admission.

"He takes this step at the instance of various friends, with the concurrence and countenance of a number of Catholic gentlemen whose names have been transmitted to him and with the approbation and good will of the Right Rev. the Bishop of the Diocese.

"The House which he has taken for the purpose, is within 5 minutes walk of the Oratory, with garden and land, and capable of accommodating as many boys as are likely to be intrusted to his care.
"The house will be committed to the management of an experienced lady, as Matron; and the School-Room and its Masters will be under the superintendence of Father Darnell."

TERMS £80 per annum

Edgbaston Catholic School
Head Master – The Rev. Fr. Darnell, of the Oratory
There are two vacations: one of seven weeks in the Summer, the other of three weeks at Christmas. "

Right: Edward Bellasis, Serjeant-in-Law at the House of Lords, was hugely influential in helping Newman to found the School.

When Newman joined the Catholic Church in 1845, he had been attracted by the figure of St Philip Neri (1515–95), known as the Apostle of Rome. In the 1550s, young men of Rome gathered around him for prayer, devotional exercises with music (from which the musical term *oratorio* derives), spiritual reading and discussion as well as local pilgrimages. His followers acquired the name of the room in which they met with him – the Oratory. Neri's unconventional ways and train of followers aroused suspicions about his orthodoxy under the severe reforming popes of the era, but as an old man his influence reached cardinals and popes.

Below: An early photograph of Oratory boys in the Cloisters at the Birmingham Oratory, Hagley Road and (above left) the Cloisters today.

Above and above right: The Oratory's first Head Master, Father Darnell and first 'Dame' Mrs Frances Wootten.

The spirit of St Philip and the lack of regimentation in the religious institution which he initiated appealed to Newman and he felt that St Philip's Congregation was the path for him in his new communion. In *The Idea of a University*, he comments "whether or not I can do any thing in St Philip's way, at least I can do nothing in any other".

It was Newman's educational influence and prestige to which the group of promoters in London wished to attach their school project. The intention that the school should be staffed by lay teachers was a point which harmonized with Newman's emphasis on the importance of the laity in the Catholic Church.

Father Darnell assumed control as Head Master from Christmas 1858. The writer Paul Shrimpton describes him as "active, capable and self-confident, with a taste for school-mastering". He appeared an ideal choice as Head Master, especially as he had some years earlier struck up a close friendship with Mrs Frances Wootten, who was appointed as 'Dame' to fulfil Newman's intention to incorporate a gentler feminine influence in the running of the School. Mrs Wootten was the convert widow of an Oxford doctor. She formed an integral part of Newman's vision of a softer quality of control compared with that prevailing in contemporary public schools. In their respective strong personalities lay the seeds of a conflict that was soon to break out. Newman described them as "the two pillars of my undertaking".

Darnell appointed Robert Moody (1823–1907) as his Second Master in February, 1859. Other members of his staff were – Edward Ransford (1835–1901), tutor and usher, later replaced by James Marshall (1829–89), Abbé Rougemont, Mathematics master (from 1861), Henry Oxenham (1829–88), tutor (from August 1861).

It has been traditionally held that The Oratory School opened its doors on 2nd May, 1859, but there is evidence to indicate that the true date of the foundation should indeed be 1st May, 1859. The first boys arrived on the first day of May in that year, in readiness to begin work on the following day. The confusion may well have arisen from the fact that 2nd May is the feast of St Athanasius, a saint to whom Newman was particularly devoted and whose day was kept with some solemnity in the School.

The School's first home was a house at 97 (now 215) Hagley Road, not far from the Oratory. In an issue of the *Magazine* in 1901, an Old Boy recalls that:

> "everything was carried on at 97, which had a long strip of garden which served as a sufficient playground. It had a good racquet court at the lower end … The playground was also distinguished by a barrel on the top of a long pole, where Wilberforce kept pigeons, and in the front garden upon Hagley Road were two conspicuous birch trees … The boys went to the Oratory for Mass only on Sundays, the week-day Mass being said at 97 in a small room at the top of the house."

Mrs Wootten resided at No 97 with Ransford as a live-in tutor. Nine boys arrived for the opening of the new school in May 1859 and they lodged with her.

When the School reopened for the Michaelmas term 1859, numbers had grown to 14. In 1860, Darnell leased property in Monument Road, around the corner from the Oratory house, which possessed eight acres of meadowland. This became 'Bosco', the School's first playing field. He also leased a house at 6 Vicarage Road, across the Hagley Road from the Oratory. This was to be

Right: St Philip Neri (1515–95), Newman's great spiritual inspiration.
Cardinal Newman said of him: "He came to the Eternal City and he sat
himself down there, and his home and his family gradually grew up around
him … reading the hearts of those who came to him, and curing their
souls' maladies by the very touch of his hand …"

This is a copy of a painting by Italian artist Guido Reni (1575–1642) that
hangs in the Rome Oratory. It has been with the School throughout its history,
and first hung in the Chapel at Edgbaston and then at Caversham (below).
It now hangs in the Chapel at Woodcote.

the base for a new Dame, Miss Elinor French, to allow for
increasing numbers. A new chapel for the boys was built,
connected to the main church, where the boys attended
daily Mass. A large room on the ground floor of the
Oratory house became the main schoolroom and a space
at the rear, supplemented by an adjoining field, became
the main play area. So the activities and focus of the
School began to coalesce around the Oratory house, the
boys being escorted to the School in the morning and
returning to their houses in the evening. Newman wanted
to build central school buildings between the Oratory and
adjacent houses recently acquired and gradually close the
School around the Oratory. Such a development would
bring the boys into closer contact with the Oratory, which
would please Bellasis and his colleagues in the venture.

At this stage Newman was little in evidence in the
School. Initially, during the summer of 1859, there had
been a reason for that, when he was acting as Editor of
The Rambler, a journal founded in 1848 as an organ of lay
Oxford converts. Newman's association with the journal
and with its reputation for challenging thinking on the
position of the Catholic Church in England, helped to
arouse suspicions in the hierarchy about Newman's

orthodoxy and the soundness of his allegiance to Rome.
These suspicions later rubbed off on the School.

By the middle of 1860, numbers in the School had
risen and there were discussions about expansion of the
buildings. All seemed to be going well, but trouble
loomed ahead. Darnell began to develop his own agenda
without reference to Newman. Indeed he discouraged
Newman from involving himself in the School.
Reviewing this situation in retrospect, Newman wrote to
Henry Wilberforce in January, 1862: "I have been more
and more elbowed out of the school – till I knew nothing
about any thing." But Newman trustingly felt that Darnell
needed time to establish matters in the School.

During the course of 1861 Newman began to be
concerned about Darnell's running of the School,
particularly: the lack of discipline, poor academic

DUKE OF NORFOLK

An important entrant in 1861 was Henry Fitzalan-Howard, the 15th Duke of Norfolk, who maintained a strong commitment to Newman, the School and Oratorian ideals throughout his life. Duke Henry was the most prominent public Catholic figure in Victorian England. He undertook a variety of philanthropic endeavours to rejuvenate Catholicism throughout the country, including founding the Catholic college of St. Edmund's, Cambridge. Duke Henry set up the Oratory School Society for Old Boys in 1874 and served as its first president. He instituted the Norfolk Prizes that still remain the top awards for academic distinction in the School. During his lifetime he was generous in support of the School and the long connection between the Norfolk family and the O.S. was born.

standards and religious tone in the School. He aired these concerns gently in a letter to Darnell in August, 1861. Darnell ignored this letter and was becoming increasingly autocratic in his direction of the School, trying to curb the influence of Mrs Wootten.

Crises are often precipitated by seemingly trivial events. This was the case in what has become known in Oratory School annals as the Darnell Affair when, in December 1861, Mrs Wootten took a rather sickly boy, Francis Cholmeley, into Birmingham for an outing that she felt would do him good. As a consequence Darnell, who objected to Mrs Wootten's position and influence in the School, issued new rules curtailing her authority and restricting the free access of boys to her.

Mrs Wootten appealed to Newman, placing him in a quandary. He needed both of these figures to retain the confidence of parents. Newman sought a compromise, whereby each would have different spheres of responsibility, Darnell as Head Master of the senior boys and Mrs Wootten as matron of the junior boys, with Mrs Wootten deferring to Darnell in any dispute. Her commitment to Newman and to the ideals with which he aimed to imbue his foundation is reflected in a letter she wrote in 1861 to Minna, Duchess of Norfolk, mother of Duke Henry: "If Fr Newman is lent to this school for some weary years to come, he will doubtless go on in his hidden way until he has made of it something very

pleasing to St Philip and by simple gentle easy ways will form his Boys for useful manhood."

Darnell rejected this solution and refused to accept any compromise, demanding the instant resignation of Mrs Wootten. The crisis was threatening to split the Oratory fathers and Newman was forced to choose between the two warring personalities. In a meeting of the Oratory fathers, it was proposed that Darnell remain in position until Easter 1862 with Mrs Wootten taking leave in the interim. Then Darnell revealed that he was determined to resign and that some of the teaching staff had signed a letter of resignation in his support. Newman accepted the resignations including that of Miss French, leaving Mrs Wootten as the sole Dame. Darnell departed from the Oratory and resigned from the Congregation with effect from 15th July, 1862.

The root cause of discord between Mrs Wootten and Father Darnell was that she was vigorously opposed to the plans of the Head Master and some others of the staff to relocate the School away from Edgbaston.

Newman was now left to sort out the problems at the School, strongly supported by Serjeant Bellasis and James Hope-Scott. The urgent task was to engage new staff, a task which was made easier when two of those who had resigned in support of Darnell, Rougemont and Marshall, made their peace with Newman. Miss Sophia Mitchell, a former governess of a friend of Newman's, replaced Miss French. Thomas Arnold, son of the famous Head Master of Rugby School, agreed to leave his post at the University in Dublin and to join Newman's venture in Birmingham, as First Master. Richard Pope, Vice Principal of St Bernard's School, Gibraltar, accepted the post of Second Master. He was to remain on the staff for 38 years, becoming one of the Oratory School's great characters, a much loved and respected schoolmaster, known affectionately as 'Pa Dick'. Richard Pope's brother, Thomas Alder Pope, also joined the staff. He later became a member of the Oratory community and was ordained a priest in 1869.

School of the Oratory, Edgbaston.

INSTITUTED IN 1859.

Circumstances having suddenly made it necessary to re-arrange the educational staff of the School, it has been thought respectful to the Parents and Friends of the Pupils to issue a list of Masters, &c., as they stand at present.

PREFECT OF STUDIES AND DISCIPLINE—FR. J. H. NEWMAN, D.D.

PREFECT OF DORMITORIES AND PLAYGROUND—FR. WM. NEVILLE, B.A., of Winchester School, and Trinity College, Oxford.

SPIRITUAL DIRECTORS—FR. STANISLAS FLANAGAN and FR. HENRY BITTLESTON.

FIRST MASTER—PROFESSOR ARNOLD, M.A., of Rugby and Winchester Schools; late Fellow of University College, Oxford.

SECOND MASTER—RICHARD POPE, Esq., late Vice-Principal of St. Bernard's College, Gibraltar.

THIRD MASTER—M. L'ABBÉ ROUGEMONT, B.A., of the University of Paris.

Assisted by Two Tutors, Members of Universities; and by French, Music, Drawing, and Drill Masters.

A Lady, who has had great experience in the care of young persons, and is well known to the friends of the Fathers, takes charge of the House, lately occupied by Miss French.

The Term commences on the 24th of this month.

JOHN H. NEWMAN.

January 13, 1862.

Left: The revised prospectus of 1862.

Below: The School's first home at Hagley Road, Birmingham.

Ambrose St John agreed, despite his indifferent health, to step in as the assistant to Newman. Newman was now officially in charge of the school founded on his prestige and educational vision, bearing the title of Prefect of Studies. All that remained was to see whether this speedy rebuilding of the fledgling foundation was supported by the parents. Some of these, for example Lord Charles Thynne, Sir John Simeon and Charles Scott-Murray, were public school educated converts. They were dismayed at the turn of events and at the departure of Darnell. They felt that this marked the end of their hopes for a Catholic public school in England. However Newman replied firmly to Scott-Murray "that to have succumbed [to Darnell's ultimatum] would have been unjust, ungrateful, cowardly, disloyal to the Oratory, and utterly disgraceful".

A new prospectus had been sent to the parents over Newman's name and dated 13th January, 1862.

The new school term began at the end of January and Newman was greatly relieved when all the pupils turned up as he had been prepared for "not more than a sprinkling of boys". With the uncertainty about the return of the boys behind them Newman and St John set about arranging matters in the School. Newman was

able to look back with relief on this sudden storm in the School's progress and its swift resolution.

A boost to morale was the commissioning of the new schoolroom which had been built between the Oratory house and the houses on the Hagley Road that had been purchased (Nos 67, 68) with an inheritance of Ambrose St John's. It was at this point that 97, Hagley Road was given up and 21 and 22, Plough and Harrow Road, behind the Oratory, were taken into the expanding campus. No 21 was used as accommodation for masters and for their common room. In 1870 the boys housed in No 22 were transferred to St Joseph's dormitory in the Oratory house and the vacated space was turned into studies for senior boys.

St John's diary for 1862 records an improvement in order and religious observance by the boys as well as in academic achievement. Things were beginning to settle down as the Summer term opened. There were four new entrants after Easter and the new regime was having an effect.

Another area in the School's activity that needed attention was religious instruction. An incident involving an acrimonious dispute between Bishop James Brown of Shrewsbury and Serjeant Bellasis illustrates how important this area of the School's life was to its reputation. It also illustrates the nature of the damaging rumours about the School that were abroad at the time. The School's aims and existence were to arouse suspicion in the English Catholic world well into the 20th century.

Bishop Brown met Edward Bellasis on a train when the latter was on his way to visit his sons at the School in October 1862. Ambrose St John reported the exchange between the Bishop and Bellasis to Newman as follows:

Below: Newman's letter to the 'Masters, Tutors and Dames of the Oratory School', 1862.

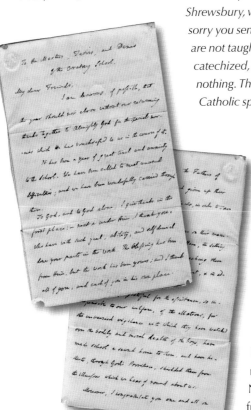

"On his way here he met the Bishop of Shrewsbury, who came out at once, 'I am very sorry you send your boys to that school … They are not taught their religion – They are not catechized, a mere half [hour] a week is nothing. The school is not conducted in a Catholic spirit', etc. etc. etc. Bellasis got very warm, so did the Bishop."

Bellasis wrote to the Bishop, who replied that his information came from two parents who did not find the School in the matter of religious instruction "like our other Catholic schools". The Bishop said that he was not surprised since the instruction was given by converts.

The crisis of the Darnell Affair, the first of many in the School's history, had been weathered but must have placed a great strain on Newman for whom there were further trials ahead. A great support to

him was Ambrose St John. Newman's involvement in the School was close, as St John's diary reveals, but his creative powers were not diminished. It is worth recalling that during the 1860s Newman wrote the *Apologia* and the *Dream of Gerontius*, prepared other works for publication, penned numerous letters, dealt with a succession of visitors at the Oratory, looked after the finances of the School, and kept abreast of all ecclesiastical happenings.

Towards the end of 1862, the situation had been steadied and in December, 1862 Newman wrote a letter which he addressed to the "Masters, Tutors, and Dames of The Oratory School" and which is a prized possession of the School's Archives. It reads:

"My Dear Friends,

I am desirous, if possible, that the year should not close without our returning thanks together to Almighty God for the special mercies which He has vouchsafed to us in the course of it.

It has been a year of great trial and anxiety to the School. We have been called to meet unusual difficulties, and we have been wonderfully carried through them.

To God, and to God alone, I give thanks, in the first place:- next, and under Him, I thank you, who have with such zeal, ability, and self-denial done your parts in the work. The blessing has been from Him, but the work has been yours; and I thank all of you, and each of you in his own place …"

The letter encapsulates Newman's ambitions for the School and his educational principles. It also exudes his relief that the institution had survived this major test in its early years. He knew that in the event of failure there were many who were ready to blame him, though no sense of anxiety about that comes through its lines.

CHAPTER TWO

NEWMAN AND ST JOHN TAKE OVER

Edgbaston, 1862–72

"Oratory boys have a distinctive ethos, something that descends from Newman's idea of a Christian gentlemen."
– Monsignor Ronald Knox

During the decade after the Darnell Affair, Newman and St John guided the School to stability. They encouraged activities that would bring them, the Fathers of the Oratory and the teaching staff, into closer contact with the boys. The resulting ties of friendship allowed them to exercise a Philippine influence, characterised by gentle control and guidance over their charges.

Opposite: The altar of St Athanasius in the Church of the Birmingham Oratory.

Right: Edward Bellasis (O.S. 1862–70), son of Serjeant Edward Bellasis.

Ambrose St John had set about reorganising and reinforcing religious instruction in the School. He and Newman were acutely aware of the damaging rumours in circulation that the religious life of the School was not as people expected it to be. At the same time they sought to stiffen academic standards by introducing regular examinations under the direction of external examiners.

The schoolboy diary of Edward Bellasis runs from 1864 to 1870 and gives detailed glimpses of church services, sporting activities, academic arrangements, and treatment of illnesses, from the schoolboy's point of view. In his diary for July 1865, he writes of the examinations:

"(13th) The 3rd form had to do two papers, the first was a piece of prose, English, which we had to turn into Latin prose, it was about Scipio Africanus. The second paper was a Virgil paper, in which we had to construe a rather hard passage in the third book of the Aneid [sic], line 356 to 368 (inclusive both ways), finished them about 12.15.

"(15th) Had a Cicero paper to do, and also an historical one, the former were questions from the

Left: The Latin Play was first performed in 1865 and became a highlight of the School year. It gradually lapsed after Newman's death in 1890, but was revived for a final time in 1909.

beginning of De Senectute *within what we had ever done of Cicero, which was not much, being only three pages, the latter was a paper in which one or two questions were asked, namely to give a history of the Norman Invasion and the causes which led to it, and give the characters of Edward the Confessor, Harold and William; my account constituted in length three pages."*

On 18th July Bellasis recorded the culmination of these tests showing the importance they had been given by the authorities at the end of term 'break-up':

"At 8 o'clock all the boys came into the refectory. Dr Newman was in the chair. Father Ambrose and Father William (Neville) on each side of him. After the overture to the 'Barbiere di Seviglia' [sic] had been performed by two violins, one tenor, two violoncellos, and a double bass, Father Ambrose opened the proceedings. He showed the marks of each examination for the Norfolk prize, the marks for arithmetic, Euclid, Homer, and all the other subjects for the prize … There were also five pounds for the next most successful competitor, whose name was Sparrow. There were also other prizes for things not in any way connected with the Norfolk Exhibition. Then after vocal and instrumental music,

and after the feast was over, prayers were said in St Philip's Chapel, and we all went to bed."

Written reports to the parents dwelt on the boys' developing characters. In July, 1864 Newman reported to Bellasis's parents:

"I should have liked to have told you myself about your boys. You know they all got prizes. I was quite surprised at E's papers – they are wonderfully creditable. Neither he nor B. had quite satisfied me in the course of the term, but the examination showed me that they had really made progress."

The religious life of the School received great emphasis alongside that given to St Philip. Edward Bellasis recorded retreats and the observance of the Easter ceremonies. When the temperature fell in winter, the playground became a skating rink. The adjacent ball-court was flooded and was likewise used for skating.

In his *Memoirs on the late Cardinal Newman and the Oratory School*, Henri La Serre, the French master, recorded that: "the top side of the playground, just against the long wall, was divided into small plots, and anyone who had a taste for gardening could please himself. Most of the boys used to sow or plant flowers." He also mentioned that:

"Besides cricket, football, and every sort of athletics, [the boys] were allowed to procure little pets, such as hawks, doves, guinea pigs, white rats and the like, on the express understanding that they would keep and feed them well."

One prominent activity in the School's year was the Latin Play, staged for the first time in 1865. For example, Edward Bellasis wrote in April, 1866 that preparations were being made for the performance of the *Pincerna*, Newman's adaptation of Terence's *Eunuchus*, in which

Bellasis himself had a part. Newman adapted the texts of the chosen plays for the boys and supervised the rehearsals.

The performance of Terence's *Phormio* was a feature of St Philip's Day 26th May, 1865. This feast day was regularly celebrated with some solemnity in the School. The year 1865 also saw the first awarding of the prestigious Norfolk Prize, which helped Newman and Ambrose St John to put the focus on academic standards, and, in addition, the first staging of the Athletic Sports.

Below: Phormio.

Left: The earliest known photo of an O.S. cricket team, 1867. William Sparrow is on the far right.

Above: Cricket practice on the playground behind the School.

Opposite: The O.S. first played against Beaumont in 1867. This marked the start of a long and fierce cricketing rivalry between the two schools that continued for nearly 100 years.

Music played an important part in the life of the School. The *Magazine* of April 1910 quotes Newman on the subject of Music in the School in 1865:

"To my mind music is an important part of education, where a boy has a turn for it. It is a great resource when he is thrown on the world; it is a social amusement, perfectly innocent; and, which is so great a point, employs his thoughts … It is often a great point for a boy to escape from himself, and music enables him."

The emphasis in the running of the School was strongly on academic performance and correct behaviour, underpinned by encouragement and sympathy. Each boy's progress and achievement were monitored in interviews with Newman and St John.

Organised sports developed in the School during the 1860s and early 1870s. William Sparrow was a long-time supporter and devotee of O.S. cricket since his days in the School. He published a series of articles in the *Magazine* on the History of Oratory Cricket:

"My first personal acquaintance with the Oratory was in the Autumn of 1863, and then all the lovers of cricket were still overwhelmed by the dire disaster

which had befallen our eleven the preceding summer, at the hands of the Oscott second eleven. It had been a complete rout, and the general opinion among us brats [O.S. slang for fags] was that any attempt to reverse the decision would be hopeless. In those days we played at 'Bosco', as we named a piece of rough ground some way down Monument Lane, situated just behind where the poor school stands, and the state of the wickets, the length of the grass, and the unevenness of the ground would have cast your present [1893] worthy captain into a fit at the mere sight. There was no attempt at scientific play, nor indeed was it possible when every other ball shot or kicked …"

In 1868 Bosco was given up and a new ground called 'Prado', adjoining the Gymnasium ground on the Portland Road, was used. In 1872 Prado had to be relinquished for the building of the railway line to Harborne. It was replaced by Ravenhurst, a farm in the Chad Vale near Harborne. It became the School's legendary sports ground until the School moved to Caversham Park in 1922. The ground was initially leased in 1873, but was purchased in 1892 with the help of the Duke of Norfolk.

Beaumont Lodge was a mansion near Windsor presented to the Jesuits in 1854. It was used as their

novitiate until the latter's transfer to Roehampton in 1861 when the building was turned into a school. A fixture with Beaumont in 1867 marks the beginning of a long cricketing rivalry. In 1926, the contest between Beaumont and The Oratory was accorded the privilege of a fixture at Lord's. This continued until the closure of Beaumont in 1966, when the College's place was taken by Downside.

In June 1896, William Sparrow explained in an article in the *Magazine* how the sport of football evolved in the School:

"… as the old O.S. game was neither Rugby nor Association, and was not played elsewhere, Oratory boys were unable to join in football away from the Oratory. [There] was no passing, but, on the other hand, individual dribbling was much encouraged, and charging was a marked feature of the game. Moreover there was no crossbar to the goals, but if the ball was sent between the lines of the post anywhere from the earth to the zenith it counted as a goal."

An account of a new boy's first day given by Henri La Serre gives some indication of the atmosphere in the School during this period:

"Patrick Waldron was a good boy, the son of the then Lord Mayor of Dublin … The very first morning he came, Patrick, as soon as the bell for play rang at 11 a.m., emerged in the open ground with quite a pleasant air. Gradually, the boys gathered round him, just to have a look at that newcomer, from St Patrick's land and judge for themselves. After a few questions about name and age and the like, as is customary with boys, when a new school fellow makes his first appearance, one among the crowd shouted: 'Pat, jump on that barrel, and dance us a

jig.' There was a barrel close by. Patrick most humorously complied with the request, and after having sung a verse, began to perform the jig called for, to the greatest delight of his comrades …

"Encouraged by their clamorous 'encore' he sang a second verse, and the jig went on at a tremendous pace. Whilst he was all heart and soul in it, kicking his heels like fun, presently some fellow flung a rotten apple at him, and caught him on the nose. Good Lord! Pat who had seen the man, jumped, as quick as lightning, from his barrel, forced

his way through the crowd, chased the fellow, who was much taller than him, and gave him such a sound thrashing as to make him call for mercy.

"The day after, Patrick Waldron was elected, by common consent, captain of Games of his Division."

One new member of staff, who came in September 1867, was the poet Gerard Manley Hopkins. He had become a Catholic while studying at Oxford and had been received into the Church by Newman, to whom he looked as his mentor. When John Walford, a former master at Harrow and Eton, decided to leave the staff to prepare for ordination, Newman offered his position to Hopkins who taught the Fifth Form of five boys and had two other advanced pupils. He was in charge of their games. He wrote that he was "very fond of my 'spiritual children', which fondness the fattest and biggest has repaid by laming me at football with a kick on the ankle". It was clear by the end of the year that he was not cut out to be a schoolmaster. Also his commitments as a member of staff left him little time to concentrate on his writing interests and he wished to pursue his religious vocation, which he did finally with the Jesuits. So he gave notice to Newman that he would be leaving after Easter 1868.

Newman wrote to him in May, 1868:

"I am both surprised and glad at your news. If all is well, I wish [to] say a Mass for your perseverance. I think it is the very thing for you. You are quite out, in thinking that when I offered you a 'home' here, I dreamed of your having a vocation for us. This I clearly saw you had not, from the moment you came to us. Don't call 'the Jesuit discipline hard', it will bring you to heaven. The Benedictines would not have suited you.

We all congratulate you.

Ever Yrs affly John H Newman."

Left: Gerald Manley Hopkins taught at the School for two terms from September 1867.

Right: Two long-serving masters, E. Alleguen known as 'Hex' (right) and R.V. Pope, 'Pa Dick' (far right).

Magazines were to play an important role in School life. William Sparrow wrote about them in the *Magazine* of 1895:

> *"At the beginning of 1868 … two of the fifth form joined with one of the junior masters, Mr J. Scott Stokes, in editing a weekly journal called* The Early Bird *or* The Tuesday Tomtit … *An opposition journal came out on the Sunday following the first appearance of* The Tuesday Tomtit. *It described itself as* The Weekly Wasp, *and was of decidedly spicy not to say libellous character. It began by a scathing attack on the Tomtit's leading article, which had been written by Mr Stokes, and spared nothing and nobody in its denunciations. Only one copy was circulated in an ordinary exercise book …*
>
> *"Of course, this warfare gave great pleasure to the school generally, more especially as the articles were supposed to be anonymous in both papers, but everyone knew that Mr Stokes was the author of the attacked 'leader'."*

Reminiscences from Old Oratorians in the *Magazine* record many instances of unruly behaviour in class,

showing that schoolboys have not changed over time and that keeping order in a class is an art that involves the establishment of respect for the teacher. Charles Vaughan wrote:

> *"[The First Form] had for their master in my day Mr All[e]guen or 'Hex', as he was always called, why, I never heard. How he did like making a joke, and how he enjoyed the groans which invariably followed. He was a dear old man, and we liked him. He and Mr Pope, or 'Pa Dick', as we familiarly called him, were the two oldest masters at that time. One of his great sayings was: 'Vaughan, Vaughan, what is your unhappy name? At it again, as per usual!! …'"*

Vaughan continued his *Magazine* reminiscences of classroom discipline:

> *"The greatest bit of audacity I ever saw was one afternoon at geography class. I think it was a boy who had somehow managed to get hold of some pepper, blew it from his hand towards the master's face (a charming man, too, who went by the nick-name of 'toe-nails') when he thought he was looking the other way,*

but he selected the wrong moment, and also made a bad shot, and was rewarded next morning at mid-day by taking part in a procession to the small school-room, where he was 'tanned', as we used to call it."

La Serre had some interesting observations on the writing of lines:

> *"As boys will be boys, it is not a wonder if some of ours were always ready to use their industry in completing their impositions as quick as possible. One of them had invented for that purpose, a kind of penholder in the shape of a rake, with no less than five pens, figuring the teeth. There was no patent for that new system of writing, so it was soon adopted at large."*

In the 1860s uncertainty hung over the School's prospects. On 16th January, 1865 Propaganda at Rome, confirming a decision of the previous year made by the English bishops at the instigation of Cardinal Wiseman, issued an instruction to the same bishops to dissuade parents from sending their sons to Protestant universities. Even though most of the hierarchy were pleased with this outcome, some were not entirely enthusiastic about a directive, which, in effect, prevented the School (as well as other Catholic schools) from preparing its pupils for attempting entry to Oxford and Cambridge.

The matter became intertwined with a dispute over a proposal by Newman to set up an Oratory in Oxford. When Cardinal Barnabò, the Cardinal Prefect of Propaganda, wrote to Newman on 11th March, 1867 his letter contained reference to these two points, which were causing concern to members of the English hierarchy, as well as to people in Rome.

Newman said he accepted and promised to abide by his guidance. However there was nothing to prevent a parent who was determined to ensure their son's entry to Oxford or Cambridge from arranging private tuition for

that purpose. When this happened the School and Newman were criticized.

Parents were being discouraged from sending their sons just as the School was in need of more boys to become financially viable. Suspicion in Rome over Newman's influence and intentions was affecting the venture. Newman wrote to James Hope-Scott in March, 1867:

> *"We must be ready to give up the school and I think it will come to this. For how can we say that we do*

Above: Cardinal Wiseman was instrumental in getting the Vatican to recommend that Catholics should not apply to Protestant universities. This presented Cardinal Newman with a dilemma as it meant that the School could not prepare boys for entry to Oxford and Cambridge.

Above: O.S. boys in the playground.

not indirectly prepare for Oxford, while *we teach classics and mathematics, and* those *parents send their children to us especially* who will not *pledge themselves* not *to send their boys to Oxford?"*

So Newman asked Ambrose St John to go to Rome to clear up the misunderstandings and rumours surrounding him and the School. Newman gave him a *Memorandum on the Oratory School* "to be presented to Propaganda on behalf of the School of the Oratory by Fr Ambrose St John", in which he outlined the events and rationale behind the foundation of the School and also tried to address some of the charges being made against it. St John went to Rome, accompanied by Father Henry Bittleston. He was not only Newman's trusted friend and confidant, but also the Head Master of the School and a linguist. Hence he was an appropriate emissary.

The visit achieved its purpose of allaying the suspicions of Newman's loyalty to the Catholic Church. St John was able to present factual evidence to Cardinal Barnabò that helped to dispel the rumours surrounding Newman. The threat to the School receded. The visit had cleared the air.

31

CHAPTER THREE

A Sure Hand in Charge of Newman's Legacy

Father John Norris, 1872–1911

"Fr John Norris orders all things for the School"

– Instruction of Newman to the 'Fr Secretary of the School', dated 10th February, 1869.

Opposite: Three Edgbaston boys.

Right: This painting by E. Burrough-Johnson 'depicted Father Norris as all had known him, albeit, in one of his gentler moods'.

John Norris was an unlikely person to fit into the scene at Edgbaston. He was a Lancastrian by birth, from a completely different background to the people whom he joined there. He came from recusant stock in that most loyal of counties to the old faith. He had gone to Ushaw College, near Durham, to study for the priesthood, but his student days at Ushaw were cut short by poor health. He came to the Birmingham Oratory in 1864, where he acted as resident sacristan. In 1865 he joined the Community and on September 24th, 1869 he was ordained priest by Bishop Ullathorne, although prior to this he was frequently referred to with the title 'Father'.

John Norris was proud of being a North countryman and, on arrival in the Edgbaston atmosphere, did not immediately feel in his element. He lacked a university degree, although he knew both Latin and Greek, teaching and examining both at the O.S. Nevertheless Newman believed he possessed a Philippine understanding in him and encouraged him to stay. Newman's judgment was to be proved correct and vindicated.

Ambrose St John's health was giving cause for concern at the start of the 1870s. He was an asthmatic and had spent some time in St Moritz to recover his strength. The boys had begun to notice that his behaviour was becoming erratic. For example, Lord Edmund Howard, younger brother of Duke Henry, wrote to his mother in October, 1870:

"'He of the Ambrosial locks' has been awfully queer lately, he makes two or 3 new rules a day, and this morning he came up to our dormitory and ran up and down roaring and yelling like a bear with a sore head and then he got the big bell and made us all turn out to say the Angelus during which he rang the bell."

Ambrose St John tended to take too much on himself. In addition to his exertions in the School, he had duties in the parish, he had translated from the Italian the *Raccolta of Indulgenced Prayers*, and he had travelled to Rome with Henry Bittleston in 1867 to defend Newman and the School. So it made sense for him to be given relief in the School in the form of an Assistant. John Norris became that Assistant in 1868.

In January, 1875 St John worked hard for six weeks at translating from the German, Fessler's *True and False Infallibility*, a moderate interpretation of the decree on papal infallibility from the First Vatican Council. He had undertaken this task to assist Newman. He became hyperactive and at the end of April 1875, he drove Newman to Ravenhurst and then walked in hot sun to nearby Harborne to be at the opening of the Passionist Church there. For a number of days afterwards he behaved strangely and unpredictably and was taken to Ravenhurst farm to stay. Newman and Father William Neville, together with a servant, watched over him until he was calmer. Newman then returned to the Oratory thinking all was well. Around midnight a message came that he was much worse. When Newman reached Ravenhurst, St John was already dead. It was 24th May, 1875.

Newman had now lost his great friend and supporter. He had earlier written of him in 1864 in the closing pages of the *Apologia*:

AMBROSE ST JOHN

Ambrose St John was well liked amongst pupils. A former pupil wrote:

"How we all feared him and at the same time loved him. There was some thing genial and breezy about him; a kindly cheery ring in his voice which made even the naughtiest boy feel that he was a friend ...

"He always managed to impress upon us that he thoroughly sympathised with us, and that he was interested in us and our games, and that he rejoiced when we won and grieved when we lost."

The writer also recalls one of his trademark habits:

"All old boys who were at the Oratory between 1862 and 1872 will remember the jingling of Fr. Ambrose's keys, for he always carried a large bunch and generously took care that they should announce his coming long before he was in sight. On one well-remembered occasion he forgot to bring his keys with him to the dormitory and dire were the results which followed ... A footstep was heard, a light was seen, and a shadowy form came through the door. Bang! went Corry's pillow and the candle flew out of the hands of Father Ambrose, who on this occasion had neglected to advertise his arrival by the jingling of keys!"

Above: An Old Oratorian group. Father Edward Pereira is seated in the front, third from left.

"And to you especially, dear Ambrose St John; whom God gave me, when He took everyone else away; who are the link between my old life and my new; who have now for twenty-one years been so devoted to me, so patient, so zealous, so tender; who have let me lean so hard upon you; who have watched me so narrowly; who have never thought of yourself, if I was in question."

The *Birmingham Daily Post* printed an obituary notice for Ambrose St John which included:

"[in] Father St John, the Roman Catholics of Birmingham lose a valuable friend and pastor, a man whose high character and attainments reflected honour upon the communion to which he

belonged; but the general loss is yet light to compare with that which falls upon the intimate friends and colleagues of the deceased, and especially the venerable and illustrious head of the community, for whom Father St John's death snaps almost the last link that binds him to the past."

Another loss came to Newman on 9th January, 1876 when Frances Wootten died. She was buried in the cemetery of the Oratory fathers at Rednal, the only woman to have been accorded that privilege.

Mrs Wootten was to be succeeded as Matron by Miss Emily Bowles, whose brother was Father Frederick Bowles of the Birmingham Oratory. So within the space of a few months, Newman had lost the two key figures in his relaunch of the School in January 1862.

Right: The Archives have receipts and correspondence which show how involved Cardinal Newman was in the everyday life of the School. The letter on the right is one that he wrote to the boys near the end of his life thanking them for a birthday gift.

Father John Norris had taken over the headmastership from St John in 1872. So a successor for the post was already in place. He built on the foundations that Newman and St John had laid between 1862 and 1872, but there were difficulties ahead before he was able to establish what has come now to be regarded as a golden period in the history of the School.

The first difficulty came at the end of the 1870s in the form of competition from an unexpected quarter. In 1877, Monsignor Lord Petre had set up a school at Woburn Park, Weybridge, which attracted boys from the kind of background for which The Oratory was intended in the minds of its originators. When it finally closed its doors in 1885 the Oratory School's roll benefited.

A second difficulty facing the School was finance. This was to be a perennial headache. In fact the O.S. only finally achieved a state of solvency in the later 20th century under the headmasterships of Dom Adrian Morey and Adrian Snow. The Day Book records that in 1886 the 'School of The Oratory, Edgbaston' had an overdraft facility of £1,500 at the Midland Bank, Birmingham of which £1,482/10s/6d had been taken up. Loans were extended over the years by Newman himself, by Father Edward Caswall and by others. Newman, who was ever practical in financial matters, insisted that such loans were repaid.

He kept a close eye on the financial movements of the School. The School Archives retain copies of receipts for fees signed by Newman. The latest one held is dated 19th July, 1883 well after Newman had been made a Cardinal.

In 1874 a key step was taken towards the development of a wider community of interest centred on the School. In March of that year, a notice was circulated to Old Boys, advertising a meeting at the Westminster Palace Hotel:

"It is … proposed to establish a Society, similar to those which exist in connection with other schools,

having for its especial objects the holding of Annual Meetings, and the creation of a Fund available for the contribution of Prizes, the support of the Games, and such other purposes as may seem calculated, in the opinion of the Society, to advance the institutions of the School."

The meeting convened under the presidency of Duke Henry, who was the inaugural President of the Oratory School Society, as it became known. Old Boys were later termed Old Oratorians and soon the custom developed, as is used in this volume, of referring to them by the initials O.S. (for Oratory School) allied to their years of attendance.

Below: A map of the key features of the O.S. site in 1909.

Bottom: The Oratory School. A print of the 1940s, showing the houses on the Hagley Road occupied by the School. The School Room is the brick building to the right. When The Oratory School moved to Caversham Park in 1922, its buildings were occupied by St Philip's Grammar School, for which this print was made.

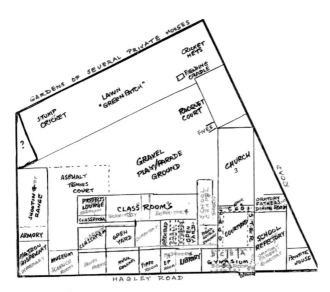

John Norris wrote to Duchess Minna, the mother of Duke Henry and Lord Edmund, in November, 1875 in the aftermath of Ambrose St John's death: "The dear old Father is I am glad to say very well – though still [feeling] very keenly his great loss – as indeed we all do. Every day makes us feel it more and in my own particular work in the School I feel it especially."

As he sought to find his style in his new position, he modelled himself on Ambrose St John, until his natural gift for schoolmastering took over. He adopted his predecessor's habit of jangling his keys to give advance warning of his approach. Gradually Norris developed a sureness of touch and the supreme confidence of the good and experienced schoolmaster. As with all respected and loved school teachers, anecdotes attached themselves to his reputation. For example, the story goes that he was once faced by a boy, who wished

to avoid attending a religious service. The boy offered in explanation 'Please Father, I've lost the faith'. To which John Norris is supposed to have replied, with the assurance of a natural school teacher, who knows and is amused by the foibles of his charges: 'Well, you'd better find it by this evening or you'll be in for a good thrashing'. His discipline was firm but gentle. No one trifled with him. His word was law.

In 1900 the *Magazine* printed some reminiscences of the School in the 1880s which give a flavour of the period:

"About 1887 there was a rage for photography. Some of the members of the fourth were up at Ravenhurst on a Sunday afternoon and one of their number suggested that they should be photographed. Pipes and cigarettes were produced and displayed to the

best advantage, and one very sporting individual had a copy of the Pink 'Un [a newspaper sports supplement] carefully arranged with the title outside so as to preclude any possibility of its being mistaken for anything else, and the group was duly taken. S, the photographer, who seems to have been a simple minded youth, having run short of chemicals thoughtfully took the plate to one of the masters and asked him to develop it, which the master did, but presented the first print the next day at 12 to Fr. John, who waxed merry at the expense of the group."

An Old Boy, Father R.H.P. Lynch, who knew him in his latter days as Head Master, recalled that:

"[we] always spoke of him as 'John' and any notice signed J.N. was far less likely to be queried than would be a Papal Encyclical today. Quiet and calm in speech, but his word was law. I never saw or heard of

any boy trying to 'play him up'. A bunch of keys at the end of a chain gave us boys a warning when 'John' was in the offing and there would be a gentle smile on his countenance, as he passed a group of us endeavouring to look completely innocent of guile …"

When a portrait of Father Norris, showing him smiling and looking avuncular, was presented to Father Edward Pereira, his successor, as part of the 1926 ceremony to mark the golden jubilee of Father Edward's connection with the School, E.P. (as he was known) commented on "[the] extraordinarily lifelike pose and deliberate poise that [the artist] had given to what was after all only a copy of a photograph. It depicted Father Norris as all had known him, albeit in one of his gentler moods."

The story goes that the boys used to watch to see whether he had placed his biretta on the back of his head or on the front, as an indication of whether he was in a good frame of mind (back) or one to be avoided (front). Gerald Headlam recalled this in his article of reminiscences about the O.S. at Edgbaston published just before he died in 1954: "It was said that when he

Above: Chinn's Tuck Shop was open on Tuesday, Wednesday and Thursday after lunch: on Wednesday only stationery could be sold but on the other days eclairs and cream cornucopias (lamb's tails and pig's ears) were the most sought after luxuries.

Right: View of the new tennis court beyond the Shed.

Far right: The Racquet Court – this game was played with a racquet ball and an ashwood bat. The bat was also used by prefects for 'spanking'.

came into the room with his biretta tilted forward one
should look out for squalls, but when it rested
comfortably on the back of the head, everything in the
garden was lovely."

After Norris assumed control, the school continued to
develop on the Edgbaston site. In 1873 a chapel was built
for the use of the school. Up until then the small
schoolroom in the Oratory house had served as a chapel,
with the boys attending important ceremonies in the
main church. In 1875 a racquet court was built against
the wall of the Church. The next year houses in Windsor
Terrace were purchased at auction and in 1880 a new St
Joseph's was built on the site of the old shed. A tennis
court was laid out on a spot occupied by two fly-poles
and a pair of parallel bars and earlier still by two trees.

Newman continued to be a presence in the School as
is shown by the fact that in 1882 he opened the library in
the former 67 (later 147) Hagley Road and he regularly
presented books to prize-winners and leavers. He was
performing the latter task just before his death on 11th
August, 1890, when he gave a copy of *The Dream of
Gerontius* to H. McE. Fox in July, 1890.

In 1879 the newly elected Pope Leo XIII raised
Newman to the rank of Cardinal. In doing so, he granted
Newman a dispensation to live outside Rome. The
granting of a red hat to someone not a bishop attached to
a see traditionally accorded that honour, usually meant
that the recipient was expected to reside in Rome, but
Newman requested and was granted permission to
spend his days in Birmingham. So the School was now
presided over by a Prince of the Church. Newman
travelled to Rome to receive the red hat in the spring of
1879. The Oratory School Society had subscribed £207
which at Newman's request had been used to buy a
complete set of High Mass red vestments. In the address of
congratulation accompanying the gift of the vestments the
members of the Society thanked Newman for the benefits
they had derived "from the privilege of your personal
influence and guidance after the wise and gentle way of St
Philip". In his reply Newman sets out his vision of the

that in part alleviated the suspicions of unorthodoxy that gossip and manoeuvring in England and Rome had cast over Newman and his work. In an address to the Mothers of the Oratory School boys by the Cardinal on 20th July, 1879 Newman commented on the interest shown by Pope Leo XIII in the School:

"When the time came for me and my friends, the Fathers who were with me, to be presented to him to take leave of him, then – though what I had asked for was a blessing upon this house, and upon the house in London, – he added of his own will, 'And a blessing upon the School.'"

Newman's death had a profound effect upon the School. That year he had been well enough to observe St Philip's Day and to officiate at the end of term break-up. The death of Newman also had a great impact not just on the Catholic community in England, but on the country as a whole and not least on the City of Birmingham. It is estimated that some 15,000 people lined the route of his funeral cortege from the Oratory to his final resting place at Rednal. Norris in his article in the *Magazine* of November 1895 marking the 50th anniversary of Newman's reception into the Catholic Church wrote:

"Whether tried by the test of nobility, intensity, and steadfastness of his work, or by the test of the greatness of the powers which have been consecrated to that work, Cardinal Newman has been one of the greatest of our modern great men …"

Above: Cardinal Newman had particular devotion to St Francis de Sales (1567–1622) who himself had been influenced by St Philip Neri. The painting shows St Francis giving the Rule of Visitation to St Jeanne de Chantal. The school motto is based on a saying by St Francis de Sales.

Top right: The coat of arms granted to the School by the College of Arms in 1998. The School had in the past used the arms taken by Newman to which he was not strictly entitled.

School's role. After a preliminary paragraph of thanks it continues, "[your] letter is the best reward, short of supernatural, for much weariness and anxiety in time past. Nothing indeed is more pleasant than the care of boys; at the same time nothing involves greater responsibility."

When choosing his coat of arms as a Cardinal, Newman selected as his motto *Cor ad cor loquitur* (heart speaks to heart). This was based on a saying of St Francis de Sales and thereby became the motto of the School, expressing its ethos. St Francis de Sales was a gentle character who influenced and reformed people by his kindness. So his approach was akin to that of St Philip and hence the sentiment was a suitable motto for the School.

The granting of the red hat to Newman by the newly elected Pontiff at the outset of his reign was a gesture

The acquisition of a sports ground at Ravenhurst in 1873 was a tremendous boost to the sporting life of the School.

Below left: O.S. Association Football XI, 1895.

Opposite: This painting by Emmeline Deane, a great-niece of Cardinal Newman, hangs in the Black Room at Woodcote. A similar portrait, also painted by Deane after the same sitting with Newman in 1884, is held by the National Portrait Gallery.

He went on to quote the generous words of Cardinal Manning in his funeral oration at the Brompton Oratory in which the Cardinal laid firmly to rest his former worries and unease about Newman's thinking: "The history of our land will hereafter record the name of John Henry Newman among the greatest of our people, as a confessor for the faith, a great teacher of men, a preacher of justice, of piety and of compassion."

It was decided to demolish the existing church and replace it with another, as a more fitting memorial to Newman.

Sport figured prominently in the life of the School under Norris. The acquisition of the ground at Ravenhurst in 1873 had given sporting activity a boost among the boys. An Old Boy recalled the sport of football in his days at the O.S. His memories record a stage in the development of the sport in the School:

"Football in the first days of Ravenhurst [1873–82] was somewhat after the manner of the famous match in 'Tom Brown'. We played a game of our own – which I think came from Winchester or

Westminster, a sort of mixture of Rugby and Association. We played in ordinary clothes, and it was not till the '80s that shorts, etc., made their appearance. In '82 Soccer was introduced; and when the ground was properly levelled, the 1st XI moved to the far end of the cricket field where the game flourished."

An impression of the kind of food served to the boys is given by the following entry in the *Magazine* during 1897:

"Beef on Sunday,
Hot for one day,
Ditto Monday,
Underdone day.
Then comes Tuesday,
Irish Stew's day.
Also Wednesday,
Warmed up ends' day.
Then Thursday,
Mince or worse day.
But on Friday,
Comes cod pie day.
Lastly Saturday,
Bones-in-batter day. "

The tradition of the Latin
Play continued under the
headship of Norris. In 1873
the *Aulularia* of Plautus
was performed. This was
also the piece chosen for
1893. The report of that
occasion, printed in *The
Tablet*, (the Catholic weekly journal)
touched on the importance of the tradition:

> "It has always been at Edgbaston the chief event of the
> year … Now that the Cardinal is gone, it remains a
> memory of his action and interest. He modelled the
> series of plays which were put into the boys' hands,
> advised and criticised the acting and the
> pronunciation, took always the keenest interest in their
> successes, and, as Old Boys will remember, kept to the
> last his kindly direction of it when his age forbad his
> touching actively on the work of the School. At a time
> when he was not often seen by the boys, and when he
> moved about but rarely, he would be assisted to see
> the rehearsals, and to say what few words might be of
> use or encouragement before the Play was finally
> produced; and hence it remains to all those connected
> with the congregation and the school, one of the
> strongest links with the memory of his last years …"

The Latin Play lapsed in the later years of Father John's
headship, but the tradition was revived with a performance
of Terence's *Phormio* as part of the 1909 events to mark the
Golden Jubilee of the School's foundation.

Lord FitzAlan, concluded a set of reminiscences of
his time: "… considering the comparatively small size of
the school – or perhaps on this very account – it is
remarkable how strong a public spirit distinguishes the
boys which it turns out". Lord FitzAlan was to become
the first Chairman of the Governing Body when it was

formed in 1931 and guided it through the troubled years
of 1941 to 1943.

Hilaire Belloc is the Old Oratorian of whom the
School is most proud. He remembered the School with
these words:

> "They [the boys] were taught to be as free – as self-
> reliant and as free – as any of the young Englishmen
> who were growing up around them in the great
> public schools; but with it all there was an
> atmosphere of healthy religion, an unconstrained
> frequency in the approaching of the Sacraments, a
> sincere faith and a high code both of morals and of
> honour, which appeared so natural and so native to
> the place, that it would have been called

*Above: Hilaire Belloc,
an Old Oratorian who
maintained close links
with the School.*

*Above left: An illustration
drawn by G.K. Chesterton
for 'But soft: we are
observed' by Hilaire
Belloc.*

Right: Father Edward Pereira in his study.

spontaneous by anyone who did not know that the founding of the school, its influence and its spirit were due to Cardinal Newman."

As the School prospered under him, Norris received honours and accolades both from within the English Catholic community as well as from the wider educational world. On various occasions he had been President of the Catholic Head Masters' Conference, to whom he often read papers on school topics, the ideas in which he presented as coming from John Henry Newman.

In February 1905, on the retirement of Father Ignatius Ryder, Father John was elected Superior of the Birmingham Oratory, and in July of the following year the degree of Doctor of Divinity was conferred on him by the Pope for his services to Catholic Education.

In 1901, the health of Norris gave great cause for concern. In May of that year he had had to undergo an operation for cataracts in both eyes. This operation was in itself successful, but was followed by a severe attack of peritonitis. For three days his life was in danger, but he pulled through and was able to accomplish ten more years of active work. For a short period in 1902 and 1903, Father Ralph Blakelock was associated with him in joint control of the School.

In 1890, Father Edward Pereira was appointed assistant to Father John Norris, but, when the latter's ill health around the beginning of the century forced the Fathers to focus on the question of the succession to him, E.P. was not the preferred candidate. They sought someone with stronger academic inclinations and chose Father Ralph Blakelock. In the event Blakelock's early death resolved the matter and E.P. became the man to succeed Norris.

John Norris resigned the headship in February, 1911. He made the announcement to the school, assembled in the Schoolroom at the end of morning lessons. He said that acting under medical advice, he was obliged to give up his duties. The comment in the *Magazine* of April 1911 in reaction to Father John's stepping down was: "[to] us of the present generation it is difficult to think of the Oratory School without him." But it continued hopefully: "Fr John still retains his position as Superior of the Oratory, so that his kindly glance still rests upon the School."

It was no surprise when the torch passed to Father Edward Pereira, for, as the *Magazine* stated: "Fr Edward, who may be said to have been for some years apprentice to the Headmaster, has now taken all the burden upon his shoulders with the cheerful courage of the true cricketer."

A period of convalescence in Bournemouth did not bring any improvement in Norris's health. He returned to the Oratory in May 1911 and died peacefully on 18th October. An era had ended and a tribute in *The Tablet* included:

"John Norris may not have been a remarkable scholar in the estimation of 'intellectuals', but he was certainly what is of far greater importance in a work-a-day world, namely, a sound, honest-minded and noble thinker, and a matchless trainer of youthful minds."

CHAPTER FOUR

Uncertain Times and Upheaval

Late Edgbaston and the Move to Caversham,
Fathers Edward Pereira and Sebastian Ritchie, 1911–22

*"… so naturally and faithfully did Fr Edward maintain the great tradition in which he was himself brought up as a boy
and served as a Master [that even] those who came after Fr John's death lived here under their united influence".*

Opposite: From the montage of Old Boys who fought in the First World War.

Below right: Stonor Park – the Pereira family home while George, Cecil and Edward attended The Oratory School.

Such was the assessment of E.P. (as Father Edward Pereira was always known) by Gerald 'Bones' Headlam on the former's first retirement from the headmastership in 1921.

Father Edward Pereira was to dominate the School's history in the two decades after the death of Father John Norris. It was remarkable that, despite the small numbers of priests in the community of the Birmingham Oratory, it gave the School two impressive leaders to perpetuate and bring forward into the 20th century, the scholastic foundation of Cardinal Newman.

Edward Thomas Pereira was born at Wolseley Hall in Staffordshire in 1866. He came from a wealthy Portuguese merchant family that had lived in Macao. His grandfather, Antonio Pereira, had sent all his sons from Macao to be educated at Stonyhurst. Edward Pereira, E.P.'s father, went to Stonyhurst in 1830 before pursuing a successful business career in Calcutta and ending up as a partner in Dent & Co in Macao. Antonio Pereira and his family moved to Mayfair, London in 1857. A year later Edward Pereira retired to England aged 41. In 1862, he married the former Honourable Margaret Stonor. E.P. had an elder sister Evy, an elder brother George and a

younger brother Cecil. Shortly after E.P.'s father died in 1872, their mother, Margaret Stonor, rented Stonor Park from her eldest brother, the 4th Lord Camoys. Stonor Park was home to the family until all the brothers had left The Oratory.

In 1876 Edward Pereira entered The Oratory School. E.P. never excelled in the academic field, but he did so as a sportsman, his great love being cricket. In 1885 he went to the Scots College in Rome to study for the priesthood. He left after a few weeks and, as the story

goes, it was on the way home that he decided that it was the Oratory where he was called to be. So he offered himself to Cardinal Newman and entered the novitiate at Birmingham in 1886. As Brother Edward, he served what was to be the last Mass celebrated by the Cardinal, on Christmas Day, 1889, after which the frail and partially sighted Newman uttered to him the words: 'Never again, Edward, never again.'

E.P. was ordained priest by his uncle, Archbishop Stonor, on 19th September, 1891. He said his first Mass the next day in the School's Chapel. He was already Assistant to Father John Norris and was much involved in the life of the School. He taught Mathematics principally and as a gifted athlete was involved with the School's games.

Evidence of his athletic ability is shown by his performances in the School Athletic Sports of 1884, in

Left: Father Edward Pereira (front right) was an outstanding sportsman and played for Warwickshire County Cricket Club.

Above: A winner in the Athletics Sports. These Sports, instituted in 1865, are still a feature of the School's life.

which he ran the 100 yards in 10.2/5 seconds and achieved a long jump of 19 feet 6 inches. This latter feat was beaten by 1 inch by W.R. Bodenham in the Athletics Sports of 31st March, 1935 in which J.W. Botting equalled E.P.'s record in the 100 yards at the same time. E.P.'s record of throwing the cricket ball 115 yards 1 foot 9 inches still holds good.

In the *Magazine* of November 1896 it is recorded:

"[we] must not omit to mention that Fr. Edward in his great interest for Cricket has had the further part of the field (at Ravenhurst) levelled, a very considerable and welcome addition, which will be found most useful, besides adding very much to the look of the ground. We beg to thank him very heartily for his generosity."

This was just one example of his offering of the family's wealth for the benefit of the School during the years of his involvement with it. His generosity was alluded to in an article on the sports ground in the *Magazine* of March 1901:

"It was again for the cricket that the present pavilion shouldered out of sight the previous make-shift. And it was no territorial ambition that made Fr. Edward a landowner, and that threatened to make him 'mine host' of 'The Old House at Home'; but, again, a generous solicitude for the cricket."

Father Edward was keen that everything should continue as it had been under his predecessor, Father John. In 1913 he oversaw the setting up of what was to become another O.S. institution, the Cadet Force, which over the years has varied its appellation. Then it was named the Officers' Training Corps (OTC), later the Junior Training Corps (JTC) and now the Combined Cadet Force (CCF). Gerald Headlam recalled this act of E.P. in his valedictory tribute in 1921 in the *Magazine* of April 1922:

"It was in the same spirit in which he supported the school games that Fr. Edward established the Oratory School Contingent of the Officers' Training Corps – more than a year before the war was ever thought of. He wanted to employ directly in the service of the country that corporate keenness and that capacity for leadership which games develop; to make boys realise that here was a form of public duty which they were invited by their country to discharge, not vaguely as an aspiration in after life, but as schoolboys and at once."

The first Commanding Officer was Edward James, who gave up the post at the start of the First World War, when

he enlisted in the Royal Warwickshire Regiment. He left the Army in 1919 with the rank of Major, returned to the O.S. for a term, before going out to Rome to study for the priesthood. He was ordained in Rome on Holy Saturday 1923. He died in 1966, the oldest priest in the Archdiocese of Cardiff. He was succeeded as Commanding Officer of the OTC by Gerald Headlam.

A Rifle Range and Armoury were erected behind the tennis court along the wall of Windsor Terrace. The cost was defrayed by a vote from the Oratory School Society. This was the last important addition to the facilities before the move to Caversham Park in 1922. In that move it was taken from Edgbaston and re-erected in its old form in the new home of the O.S.

The first Sergeant-Major was Colour Sergeant Warchus. He became an O.S. character and went with the School when it relocated to Caversham in 1922. He eventually retired in July 1932. The *Magazine* of December 1932 wrote in appreciation of his service to the School: "Many generations of old boys will remember 'Wackers' with respect and affections [*sic*], and his phrases and slogans will be much missed in camp and on the Range, where he has cleaned so many rifles and cursed so many bad shots."

Together with the destruction of the cricket pavilion by Suffragettes in 1914, there was another unexpected event at this period of the School's story, which reflected national political struggle. It is recounted in the *Magazine* of April 1922:

"On our return to School in September [1921], we were greeted with the alarming news that a robbery had occurred in the Armoury, during the holidays and four rifles and about 3,000 rounds of ammunition had been removed. The criminals have not been detected nor have the missing stores been recovered. In consequence of this disaster, the Armoury and Magazine have been provided with additional locks,

bolts and bars, and during the Christmas holidays the arms and ammunition were removed to a place of greater secrecy. It is some consolation to know that we were not the only sufferers from the political excitement which set in after the conclusion of the Irish 'Truce'. Similar robberies on a larger scale took place at the Guards' Barracks, at Chelsea and Windsor."

Above: OTC camp at Tidworth Pennings, 1913.

Left: A stalwart of the early OTC, Sergeant-Major Warchus (centre), known as 'Wackers'.

THE SUFFRAGETTES

A serious blaze damaged the house on 24th February, 1901 and fire visited Ravenhurst in a more dramatic fashion a few years later. The event was recounted in a letter written to *The Times* and published as a contribution to a discussion in the newspaper about Suffragettes in 1987. The letter reads:

"On the evening of Thursday, May 13, 1914, some of these 'wild women' [Suffragettes], as they were known, travelled to a country area called Ravenhurst, some four miles from the centre of Birmingham. The visit of these incendiaries resulted in the cricket pavilion belonging to the Oratory School, then at Edgbaston, being razed to the ground and all the framed records of outstanding exponents of the game being destroyed.

"A day or two later, on arriving at their headquarters in the city, the Suffragettes discovered that their own building had been mysteriously wrecked. Birmingham was, of course, out of bounds to the school, but Oratory boys have never been beyond a spot of 'tibbling' [i.e. breaking bounds] even when the honour of the school was not at stake."

The story goes that the original attack was made after a boy had sprinkled a bottle of red ink on some suffragettes holding a meeting on the pavement below the Schoolroom.

The culprit was believed to be a school employee, a young man called Sweeney. It was presumed that they had been taken on behalf of Sinn Féin.

As a result of its situation in the Hagley Road the School was facing the threat of being engulfed by the urban expansion of Birmingham at the beginning of the 20th century. This danger was described by Gerald Headlam in the *Magazine* of 1953:

"In my earliest years open country began about a mile west of the School, but later the land came into the market and a period of urban development set in and the fields were replaced by rows of small workmen's dwellings. This change led the Corporation of Birmingham to decide that the horse buses must be replaced by electric trams, and in spite of repeated protests signed by the residents, these soon made their appearance … these frightful trams … [made] more noise than any other vehicle in Europe, and teaching and even conversation became increasingly difficult in any building facing their route."

The theme of boys carving on panelling and the way this tradition was valued is taken up with poignancy in the *Magazine* of May 1915:

"Interesting at all times, but particularly so now when most of the carvers are serving their country in the great struggle. In the Upper School, close round the fireplace, are the names of 7, all of whom were with us in the last six years, who have already given their lives for their country."

The store that E.P. set by these names carved in the panelling of the Schoolroom is demonstrated in the colourful account that Kevin FitzGerald gave of the occasion that his difficult father took a reluctant son to Edgbaston and met Father Edward:

"A taxi from New Street took us to the school and I had a sense of utter doom as we entered it … after a while the Headmaster appeared … As we walked from one dark dank building to the next, from one battered wreck of a classroom to another, and eventually arrived at the huge apartment called the Big Schoolroom, it became clearer and clearer to me that my father regarded the Headmaster, Father Edward Pereira, as what he used to describe (rather loudly as a rule) as 'a man of no account'. It was equally clear that Father Edward was of the same opinion about him … In the Big Schoolroom my father frowned at the mass of names carved into the

panelling and said: 'A serious disfigurement'. Father Edward said: 'Money could not buy one of them'…"

FitzGerald gives his first experience of an O.S. boy:

"He [Father Edward] instantly called up a boy. 'This is FitzGerald', he said. 'Show him about.' He disappeared and the boy said 'Clear off and look after your bloody self'. I thus became an Oratory boy. I had been 'cleared-off' by Lentaigne who died of wounds as a major-general in the Second War. He was a nice man but I only found that out later [Walter Lentaigne reached the rank of Lieutenant-General and died in 1955]."

FitzGerald recalled unhappy experiences as a new boy as he tried to settle into his new unfamiliar environment:

"I survived knowing – and also saying – that a mixture of manganese dioxide and potassium chlorate would, when heated in a test tube, give off the gas oxygen. I survived knowing the Catechism backwards – the nuns had done a good job on me. But I only just survived the Headmaster's remark one morning: 'FitzGerald appears to be the only boy in 3b with a faint glimmer of intelligence.' There came a whisper from behind of a boy later to win the almost standard Oratory DSO [in his case as a colonel of tanks at Alamein]: 'Just wait a few minutes, FitzGerald; just a few minutes'. I knew by then exactly what that meant."

In the *Magazine* of the Summer Term 1972 he concluded an article of reminiscences on 'The Oratory School in the Hagley Road' with the following words that sum up his ambivalent feelings towards his alma mater:

"I have tried to live up to the reference the Man [the nickname of E.P.] gave me for my first job. 'FitzGerald was essentially a boy the whole of whose interests lay outside the normal school curriculum. He was useless at games, but may be confidently recommended for any post requiring honesty and a certain level of integrity.' Well, I got the job."

The reference E.P. gave him illustrates Father Edward's forthrightness of expression and his ability to sum up and see into a boy's character.

Two men arrived at the School during the first decade of the century who were to contribute to its history. Sebastian Ritchie joined the teaching staff in 1905 and decided to join the Birmingham community a year later. He was ordained priest in 1910. His replacement on the teaching staff was Henry Tristram, who also became a member of the Birmingham Oratory. He was ordained at the end of September 1911.

The outbreak of the First World War in August 1914 affected the School profoundly. Its strong service

tradition meant that many of its Old Boys volunteered to fight. As casualties mounted, Father Edward was obliged to announce the deaths of many whom he had taught and known in the School. This took its toll on his own health.

The strain on him must have been increased by the realisation that from 1913 onwards he was losing his sight. It was a condition that became worse with the passing years. It subsequently emerged that he was suffering from glaucoma in the left eye. Unfortunately the condition was not caught in time. In 1916 E.P.'s sister-in-law, Helen, wrote to her husband, Cecil Pereira: "E.P. turned up last night. I must say I was horrified at his appearance … I really for a moment could not believe my eyes, he says he is weak as a cat and has lost a stone in a month."

There is a story that, after the First World War, E.P. was walking down Piccadilly with Father (Dick) Lane

Above: The Big Schoolroom.

Right: Hard at work in the chemistry laboratory.

'THE MAN'

Gerald Headlam said the following about E.P.'s nickname, 'The Man':

"For many years Fr. Edward was known to the School as 'the Man'. I was never able to discover the origin of this nickname; no one could ever tell me whether it was a complimentary abbreviation of 'the Man of God', or an equally complimentary abbreviation of 'the Man of Wrath' or even 'the Man of Sin'. Its interpretation varied, no doubt, with the individual user or his circumstances at the moment, but I never knew a school nickname which described a man better."

Left: Father Pereira (on the right) in the playground.

Below left: E.P. in his final years at Caversham.

Henry Tristram (Head Master, 1930–31) wrote about the effect of the War on E.P. in his obituary notice for his immediate predecessor as Head Master. It was published in the *Magazine* of March 1939: "The years of the War imposed an immense strain upon him, and to this was added the inevitable sorrow entailed by the heavy losses among the generation of boys who had passed through his hands."

Kevin FitzGerald records a poignant scene that brings home the pain experienced by those who lost friends and loved ones in the conflict:

"The Battle of Jutland gave us a strange night at the Oratory School. We were at preparation when the newsboys were heard crying along the Hagley Road: 'Great naval disaster: special.' The Man, who invariably took first prep, sent out for a paper and said: 'There has been a great naval battle in the North Sea; we have lost many ships.' He read out some of the names and I remember after night prayers hearing Goddard crying bitterly. His brother had been a midshipman in number 1 turret on the King George V, sunk with all hands."

Fox, Helen Pereira's brother, a Benedictine monk, who had lost an eye while serving as a Chaplain to the Irish Guards during the War. E.P. could not see out of his left eye and Lane Fox could not see out of his right eye and they kept bumping into one another. They solved the problem by changing sides.

The *Magazine* of May, 1923 summarised the School's record during the First World War in the following terms:

Above: The bravery of Old Oratorians is reflected in the military medals board that now hangs in the entrance to the School at Woodcote. Together with the engraved brass tablets now in the Chapel at Woodcote, the montage of Old Boys who served in the conflict (now in the Small Hall at Woodcote) and the Chapel built at Caversham Park, it formed part of the Memorial to those Old Boys who served and fell in the First World War.

"Here it is enough to say that [the School's] old boys have distinguished themselves and brought lustre to their School in all parts of the Empire and in every walk of life. Its record during the war may be regarded as its crowning achievement, and taken as illustrating all the years that are passed over in silence.

"In spite of the small average number of boys in the School – 70 or under – no fewer than 420 old boys held officers' commissions, and, in addition eight members of staff served. It would be impossible in a small space to give full details, but suffice it to say that [87] gave their lives in the struggle and that a still larger number were wounded, many more than once.

"[there] were more than 250 'mentions in despatches' and more than 200 other honours, the most treasured of which is the brilliant V.C. gained by General Carton de Wiart."

The health and state of mind of Father Edward caused him to resign from the headmastership in 1921. Gone was the vigorous leader and games player that the School had known. His successor was Father Sebastian Ritchie whose headmastership lasted only a year. However, it was during that year that the momentous decision was taken to sever the connection with Edgbaston and that a new home was found for the School at Caversham Park, a stately home in the southern extremity of Oxfordshire on a ridge overlooking the Thames Valley and the town of Reading. It had belonged to the Crawshay family, South Wales ironmasters, who sold it to the Fathers of the Oratory for £12,500.

The War had proved to be a period of test for the School on its site at Edgbaston. For practical and economic reasons a small school could not possibly hope to survive under the changed conditions brought about by the war years. It was impossible to expand in Edgbaston and may be not even advisable to consider

FRANCE

and so it was a happy chance for the School that Father Edward should return recovered and ready to take up the reins of office again. It required someone of E.P.'s O.S. pedigree and force of personality to manage the upheaval and break with tradition which the move to the new location represented. He had in any case been convinced of the necessity of the move. So it was fortunate that his year off headmastering, combined with a journey to the Eastern Mediterranean, restored him to full vigour and he took up the reins of control from Father Ritchie ahead of the move.

On 28th April, 1922, the lands and property at Caversham were conveyanced to the Trustees. The following day Lloyds Bank granted a mortgage to them on those lands and property. Miss Gay-Smith, the Matron, under the direction of E.P., superintended the domestic details of the move efficiently.

Father Edward, as an Old Oratorian himself, would know that the Old Boys would feel the move to Caversham as a wrench. So he submitted a memorandum to a Committee Meeting of the Oratory School Society in December, 1922, which read:

"During my absence the immensely important step of moving the School to its present quarters was decided on. Father Ritchie had found this house and grounds which are admirably suited to our requirements; and the prospects for the future are very bright. Still there

Left: The most highly decorated Oratorian, Lieutenant-General Sir Adrian Carton de Wiart (O.S. 1891–8) was awarded the Victoria Cross for his command of the 8th Battalion, Gloucestershire Regiment, at the Somme in 1916.

Below: The First World War memorial in the School Chapel naming the Old Boys who gave their lives in the conflict.

that possibility in view of the spread of Birmingham. After the end of the First World War, plans were made for a Memorial at Edgbaston. These included an additional Memorial Chapel, to be built alongside the School's Chapel, and tablets bearing the names of Old Boys who had lost their lives in the conflict. These plans were put on hold once the move to Caversham Park had been decided upon and there they were then put into effect.

The headmastership of Father Ritchie was temporary

are, naturally, many points which are bound to bring a certain amount of anxiety, and the first of these, as usual, is the financial question …

"First and foremost we would urge that every Old Boy who has sons to educate, to send them to us, even at the cost of some sacrifice in many cases. This will do more than anything to ensure the well-being of the School: it will strengthen the links with the past; but beyond all, the constant recurrence of the old names will remind us that we are one and the same School as that started by our great Founder."

The reaction of Hilaire Belloc to the move of the School to Caversham was no doubt typical of that of many Old Boys. It was to be echoed by Old Boy reaction after a further move some 20 years later. Belloc began a letter, written to Mrs Reginald Balfour in January, 1922:

"He [an Oratorian Priest met in train] tells me that the place to which they think of moving the school is Caversham House near Reading … they have to go to the country or shut down the school altogether!

Below: The School moved from Birmingham to Caversham Park in 1922.

Oratory School, Back View.

Left: The Duke of Norfolk in the 2nd XI at Caversham (back row, third from left).

Opposite: Portrait of Father Edward Pereira by Simon Elwes (O.S. 1915–19).

"If that is so, the best alternative is certainly to go to the country: but I bitterly regret the loss of tradition. It seems that the odious animal, the parent, has been making a fuss about the position in town and saying it is bad for the boys, which is rubbish. It is as healthy a site as any in England … "

However Belloc did not turn his back on his Old School. He had already sent his sons Hilary and Peter to Edgbaston and, as he did when the School was there, he visited the School at Caversham to talk to the boys.

Early issues of the *Magazine* regularly published articles of reminiscences about the School in its Edgbaston days, which served to emphasise the link between its two homes. They were also at pains to highlight, by word and photograph, the fact that boys were entering the School at Caversham, who were sons of Old Boys or from families connected with the O.S.'s past at Edgbaston. One such entrant of significance was Bernard, 16th Duke of Norfolk, who had succeeded to the title on the death of his father, Duke Henry, in 1917. Duke Bernard was part of that group of Old Oratorians who knew the School both at Edgbaston and at Caversham. He was to show reassuring commitment to

it after its move to Woodcote when its survival was at its most problematic in the 1940s and 1950s.

The move to Caversham meant upheaval to many members of staff, both teaching and domestic. In December 1924, two houses at the end of the drive next to the Lodge were completed and John Bevis and Sergeant-Major Warchus moved in with their families. One still bears the notice 'The Bursar's House' indicating how under the present ownership of the B.B.C., who bought Caversham from the School, there are reminders of previous occupants. The Chapel remains as such in B.B.C. parlance even though it now contains the quarters of B.B.C. Radio Berkshire.

The members of the teaching staff who transferred from Edgbaston to Caversham were: Gerald Headlam, Barney Webb, Daniel Arkell, Auguste Schott, C.K. Brampton and H.H. Jones but there were also some who chose not to make the move.

On the second retirement of Father Edward from the headmastership, in 1929, Simon Elwes painted a portrait of him, which was presented to E.P. on behalf of the Old Boys by Lord FitzAlan on Prize Day, 1930. Father Edward then presented it to the School and it can be seen hanging in the Black Room at Woodcote today.

CHAPTER FIVE

TROUBLES AFTER THE MOVE

Early Caversham,
Fathers Edward Pereira and Henry Tristram, 1922–31

"… the spirit of the School … instantly enveloped one and forced one into the mould … [It] was good;
it was what E.P. had worked all his life for, and it took hold of one and shaped one's basic character for all time.
And what is remarkable is that it just seemed to HAPPEN without any great effort on one's part."

Denis Gibson (O.S. 1928–33)

Opposite: Duke Bernard at OTC Camp. He is seated alongside Gerald ('Bones') Headlam, who was a loyal servant of School with a break in the 1920s, from his arrival on the staff in 1901 until his death in 1954.

With the School settled in its new premises at Caversham Park, it was a problem for the Fathers of the Birmingham Oratory to monitor its day to day progress. However, in addition to the Head Master, Father Edward Pereira, there were two other Oratorian Fathers from the Birmingham community in the house. These were Father Henry Tristram, who had come with the title of Rector, and Father Philip Lynch, Assistant to Father Edward. Father Joseph (Bacchus) and Father Stanislaus (du Moulin-Browne) came down from Edgbaston every alternate week.

The move of the School's home gave an opportunity to introduce changes in its working and life, not all of them welcomed. The *Magazine* of May 1925 makes reference to these:

"We found many alarming changes in the routine; the half-holidays a week were reduced to two: on the other hand, rugger was possible almost every day, and not merely on halves. The school timetable was so formidable as to be almost incomprehensible – quite inexplicable."

The same article then went on to greet one major change with approval, namely the adoption of rugby football as the winter game. The article concluded with favourable consideration of the upheaval:

"The change here was welcomed by all, in spite of the discomforts. The brats especially found themselves in clover: naturally the exploration of so many fresh woods and pastures new offered endless delights and there were many convenient opportunities of getting lost sometimes even during school hours.

"Tempers on the whole, weathered fairly equably the storms of settling down. Now, when everything is more or less plain sailing, people are looking back on the choppy seas behind and patting themselves metaphorically on the back, amidst an orgy of mutual satisfaction and congratulation."

After the move was completed, the question of the War Memorial was raised at a meeting of the Old Boys Society in January 1923. Father Edward was asked to prepare "a definite scheme for consideration". That

61

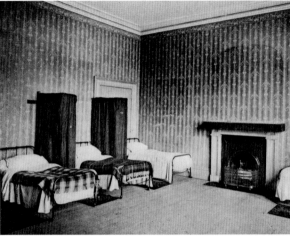

Prospectus pictures of the School at Caversham Park: a classroom (below), dormitory (left) and games room (far left).

scheme was to have three elements: tablets of white marble on a black base bearing the names of all those who fell in the War, a large tablet to be erected in the School chapel at Caversham and completion and decoration of the new Chapel at Caversham, to be the actual and lasting memorial.

A further change that was introduced to the O.S. at the beginning of its Caversham era, was the establishment of Houses. During the Lent (1923) term an experiment was found to be a success and the School was divided up into three "Houses" of about thirty boys each: "in order to give material for friendly rivalry among ourselves in work, games and athletics". The Houses were named after three eminent Oratorians, St John, Norris and Faber, and they each had their colours.

The change of the School's location had brought about much that had been in the air and Father Edward took the opportunity of his first Caversham Prize Day speech in July, 1923 to present his own manifesto of education:

"So with many hopes and great prospects we made our start … As each boy comes to the school he is a complicated problem of amazing interest: no two

boys are alike: yet the ultimate aim is the same in every case – to send out into the world a true Christian gentleman – a real man, confident and self-reliant; with a strong sense of duty, open, simple, straightforward, tactful, generous; whose 'Yes' is 'Yes' and whose 'No' is 'No'; and at the back of this a 'will power' which will carry him right through."

The sentiments expressed by Father Edward in 1923 have a feeling of being distilled from Newman, through

*. The War Memorial
Chapel was inaugurated in
1925. The School still holds
an annual service and lays
a wreath at Caversham.
Outside the Chapel lie the
graves of three boys who
died at Caversham during
the 19 years of the School's
stay there. A plaque (far
right) reminds passers-by of
this and of the original
purpose of the building.*

Ambrose St John and John Norris, and would be
subscribed to by many who have immersed themselves
in the O.S. ethos over the years. The O.S. had been
tested by the upheaval of the departure from Edgbaston
to Caversham and was to be tested more seriously in the
years to come, but it was to survive with its
consciousness of its Founder's purpose intact, albeit
latent at times.

In 1924, E.P. acquired 50 to 60 acres of land adjoining
the school boundaries to prevent the danger of being built
around. At the same time his brother, Major-General Sir
Cecil, moved into Caversham Place, a house he had built
on a plot of land next to the School. Ironically it was
demolished in the early 1950s to make way for the
construction of Caversham Park Village. So the outer
suburbs of Reading did come out to reach Caversham
Park, but by then the School was at Woodcote.

Sir Cecil took some part in the life of the School. For
example, some boys leaving without prospect of
employment would look to the Army on the General's

advice. He would arrange their entry into Sandhurst
without them taking the normal examination.

The formal inauguration of the War Memorial Chapel
took place on Easter Sunday 1925, when High Mass was
followed by the Athletic Sports and Prize Giving. In

addition to the Chapel itself, the First World War Memorial also comprised the medal case and the montage of Old Boys who fought in the conflict as well as brass plaques engraved with the names of Old Boys who lost their lives. These were executed by Mr John Waine of Caversham and now adorn the Main Chapel at Woodcote.

Shortly before this occasion Father Philip Lynch was obliged by illness to leave Caversham. His departure marked the beginning of the inevitable waning of the link between the School and the Birmingham Oratory. He nevertheless retained a close interest in the fortunes of the O.S. and until his death in 1989 provided a vital link between O.S. alumni of the Edgbaston and early Caversham eras. He also acted as Chaplain to the Oratory School Society for many years until 1968. E.P., the Head Master, Father Henry Tristram, the Rector and Chaplain, and Father Sebastian Ritchie, the Head Master of the soon to be opened Preparatory School were members of the Birmingham Community who still remained presences on the site, but the ties between the two institutions were weakening as had been bound to happen after the move away from Edgbaston.

Two important developments took place in the Summer of 1925. Firstly the numbers in the School reached 100 for the first time in its history. Secondly the Oratory Preparatory School was opened under the headmastership of Father Ritchie.

In December 1925 there had been a small fire on the second landing. It was quickly extinguished by the boys, but as a result the insurance company pointed out that the buildings were under-insured and advised a larger premium. The advice was acted upon. This was fortunate in view of what was to come in less than a year's time.

In the course of 1925 and 1926 new school facilities were built. An open air swimming pool was opened and to mark the 50 years of Father Edward's association with the School a squash-racquets court was donated by the Old Boys. Forming a part of the same celebration was

the portrait of Father John Norris, painted by E. Burrough-Johnson. All this was presented to E.P. "on behalf of the Old Boys, present generation and other friends" by Viscount FitzAlan on Prize Day in 1926.

Earlier during the summer of 1925 the gymnasium-cum-theatre had been completed at a cost of £1,000 and a cricket pavilion was started with the 1926 season in view. This together with the swimming pool cost £1,400. The Chapel received a new High Altar given by the parents of James Hasslacher, in memory of their son who was killed during the First World War at the age of 22. A new sanatorium was begun to the south of the School at a cost of £5,000. It now houses the B.B.C. archives but it was to prove invaluable in the crisis which was about to strike the School.

Above: Lord's match fixture card, 1926.

The same year of 1926 witnessed two momentous events in the life of the School. Firstly the traditional cricket match against Beaumont College was accorded the privilege of being included in the list of school fixtures played at Lord's. The first Lord's match between the two schools took place on the feast of St Philip that year.

In this match the Oratory XI won by 15 runs in a tight finish. *The Times* commented: "Needless to say, the spectators also rose to the occasion – altogether, it was quite an Eton and Harrow day on a small scale."

It became traditional over the years in which the fixture was played at the headquarters of cricket for O.S. supporters to sport a yellow carnation and Beaumont

Above and right: The Oratory and Beaumont College played at Lord's Cricket Ground in 1926 for the first time. The fixture was fiercely guarded by the School and ceased only when Beaumont closed. This was the start of a very exciting cricketing time for the school and the photographs clearly show the boys' pride at playing at Lord's.

supporters a red one. The yellow of the O.S. favour echoes the same colour in the School's flag which combines the Papal yellow and white with the Oratorian black.

The second event of 1926 was a fire that severely damaged the central part of Caversham Park at the end of the summer holidays. The account of the event, written by E.P. and published in the *Magazine* of January 1927 reads:

"On Monday, August 30th, shortly after 4.30 a.m. Frances [Dale] … smelt something burning. She went along the 'baths' corridor, and found a fire burning in the top corner of the S. E. front. The only occupants of the House were Father Edward and two maids. Brigades were summoned and the maids went to call Gray [the groundsman] and Bevis. Unfortunately the Reading Brigade was unable to send help as the House is 300 yards outside the Reading Borough. This was most unfortunate as they could have been up in a few minutes, in which case the fire could undoubtedly have been confined to the top corner rooms and £1,000 would have covered the damage whereas now it will come to about £30,000."

Sir Cecil Pereira, E.P.'s brother and the Secretary of the Oratory School Society, sent a circular letter to Old Boys to explain what had happened. He was obviously incensed at the refusal of the Reading Fire Brigade to attend the fire and the reason that they gave for this refusal, namely that they could not cross the borough boundary into Oxfordshire, in which county Caversham Park then stood.

The fire was put out by 11 o'clock that morning. Father Edward mentioned in his account of the day in the *Magazine* of January 1927 that "[the] large picture of the Madonna, which for a long time was at Edgbaston, was saved and also the portrait of the Cardinal".

Above and right: Fire gutted the central part of Caversham Park in 1926. The damage could have been far less had the Reading Fire Brigade attended the scene but they refused on the grounds that Caversham was not in their area of responsibilty.

The account of the clear-up and preparations for reopening the School are full of reassurance that clearly reflects a great deal of activity and resourcefulness.

A significant and indicative development at the end of the 1920s was the decline and disappearance of the Norfolk Prizes. These formerly prestigious awards were not presented at the Prize Givings of 1926 and 1927 and received no mention in 1928. From then on they were overlooked, until Duke Bernard revived them on his visit to distribute the Prizes in 1938. During the uncertain years of the following two decades they lapsed again but they were revived once more, again by Duke Bernard, on his visit to present the Prizes in 1966.

E.P. relied heavily in keeping control of the School on his strength of personality and his ability to read a boy's character. He knew the boys as individuals. However his increasing blindness must have taken its toll; he was nonetheless held in awe by all and his judgement of

Left: Maids cleaning up after the fire.

Right: Major-General Sir Cecil Pereira (on the right), the younger brother of E.P.

people seemed, in the eyes of many of the boys, to verge on the magical. An example of this is given by Denis Gibson who recalled an incident in 1929 when he was sent for by E.P. one evening during Prep:

> *"He kept me standing in front of him for a few moments while he looked me up and down, and then said: 'You are getting to the silly stage – stop it.' That was all. He waved me out, and I could hardly have been more anxious to obey. My respect and awe were much increased, and I trod very carefully thereafter. But of course it was so true; having been pitchforked into this gang of strong and wilful characters in No 3 Dormitory it was inevitable that I should wish to hold my own with them, and this involved various acts of daring …"*

Denis Gibson recalled E.P.'s talks to the whole School at Benediction on Sundays:

> *"He exhorted us not to flaunt our religion in public, but to be as inconspicuous as possible – 'This is a Protestant country and Catholic practices are anathema to many of our countrymen' – and always to behave as 'good CARtholic gentlemen' – he always pronounced it that way. Once in a while he would warn us of the dangers of premature sexual experience – 'IS it WORTH the RISK?' being his catchword with great emphasis on the words in capitals."*

E.P. was trying to encourage the boys to behave as Catholic gentlemen and to let their Christian behaviour speak for itself, not to flaunt their religion in public by giving themselves over to an un-English baroque spirituality.

All seemed to be returning to normal after the fire. In 1927 Gerald Headlam returned to the staff after his period at St Edmund's, Ware. At the same time as his return to the O.S. restoration work on the Central block of the School continued.

When Gerald Headlam left the staff at the end of 1923 he had handed over command of the OTC to Captain A. du Moulin-Browne, recently retired from the Army. When he retired from the post in 1924 he was replaced by Captain Justin Kane of the Irish Guards, whose two brothers also joined the staff. The three brothers, Justin, Wilfrid and Dominick virtually ran the School at this point and to the resentment of many of the boys imposed a military type of discipline. Wilfrid and Dominick left during the Michaelmas term of 1927 and Justin did likewise in the summer of the following year. At this point Gerald Headlam resumed his former command of the OTC.

In 1928 James Underhill who had been School Captain, Captain of Cricket and Captain of Rugby in his final year at school, before then entering the R.M.A. Sandhurst, was obliged to give up the idea of a career in the Army and was invited by E.P. to join the staff of his old school. Together with Gerald Headlam he provided an element of continuity and stability during the coming troubled decade. He served the School in a wide range of posts up until the outbreak of the Second World War as well as teaching English and Geography.

Just before Prize Day of 1929 the familiar statue of Cardinal Newman was erected by the wall near the Chapel entrance. This was an effective site for it as it was one of the first things one noticed on approaching the North Front by the main drive. It was presented by an anonymous donor and the *Magazine* of November 1929 claimed it was: "the original from which the statue outside the London Oratory was taken", adding that: "There was a general agreement that it was more effective than the marble one, and it certainly is an excellent likeness of the Cardinal." The statue now stands in the front courtyard at Woodcote framed by the bricked-up arch to the stable block of the Old House.

Another statue donated to the School at Caversham was that of Our Lady of Lourdes, given in 1924 by Father Denis Sheil. It stood over the porch at the North Front of the House and now resides in the Walled Garden at Woodcote near the entrance to the Old Chapel (St Joseph's). Sir Cecil Pereira in his report on the 1926 fire to the Old Boys mentioned how: "…the large statue of Our Lady, which stands on the porch of the Main entrance to the School, – it looked so calm and unmoved, – turned away from the fire with hands folded in prayer."

However, the apparent return to normality was deceptive. At the end of the Michaelmas term 1929, Father Edward resigned the headmastership. As the final farewell tribute to him in the *Magazine* of May 1930 stated:

> "[his] indomitable will had successfully overcome a serious illness some six years ago [1923]: he had hardly recuperated when the fire occurred – a blow that so far from paralysing a body so frail as his actually energised it. Both he and all of us felt that the rebuilding of the school was the grand finale to a long and devoted career in its service, and now that his eyesight was failing, the time had come for him to resign his work to more active hands."

The tribute tried to analyse the secret of his successful career:

> "In his dealing with others he had abundant common sense and believed it was not only possible but desirable for a good Catholic to possess a certain

Above: The statue of Our Lady of Lourdes, now in the walled garden at Woodcote, stood over the front porch at Caversham.

Above: The much-loved statue of Cardinal Newman that greets newcomers to Woodcote first stood by the Chapel at Caversham.

worldly 'savoir faire'. Culture and imagination were accessories to character not foundations: it was with the latter that he was most concerned, and in the most unlikely material he frequently found his ideal. Self reliance he considered was the basis of character: hence he entrusted to the boys much of the administration of the School that is usually the work of a staff. If a boy failed in his trust, he held not the boy or the principle wrong, but himself or his staff. If a boy was to fail, he argued, it was better to

do so at school and learn his lesson there than in after life where failure is so often irrevocable."

Denis Gibson commented on the end of the Pereira era:

"So this wonderful partnership [of John Norris and Edward Pereira] of over 50 years came to a sudden and shattering end in 1929. I do not suppose for one moment that I or any other of my age had the faintest idea of what had happened; we were so

completely certain of our overwhelming superiority over all the other Catholic schools that it would have taken the equivalent of several earthquakes to shake us. And of course it was the spirit of the school itself and its members which was unshakeable; everything went on just as before, because so much of the responsibility for running the school rested in its senior members … This was the great thing; the school WAS run to a remarkable degree by the boys, and there was not one who would not have fought to the death anyone who tried to make it otherwise."

Such a policy had obvious dangers, but in it can possibly be found the reason why the School and its values were to survive the two or three decades of uncertainty that now lay ahead of it. One of the dangers of such a policy is that it can open the way to bullying and brutality of punishments handed out by those boys – Prefects – allowed to administer them. Donald Cobbett recalled these when writing in 1986:

"The most severe corporal punishment was inflicted by the Prefects. This was inflicted by way of beating with a half-inch Malacca walking stick. The names of those summoned … were called out after supper, when the 'pres' had regaled themselves with small beer at the raised end of the refectory … All did not participate in this sadistic after-supper indulgence … The other corporal punishment was administered by the Headmaster [EP], it was known as a 'swishing' with a bare handful of twigs. This on the bare behind. One big chap seized the birch from the Head's hand, broke it across his knee, jumped through the window and departed the scene."

Above: Rugby football was adopted as the winter sport on the move to Caversham Park in 1922.

Left: The badge worn on the Rugby colours blazer.

For junior boys, known as the 'brats', their first year was a year to be endured and survived. They were expected to come running when a Prefect shouted out 'BRAT' for a boy to run an errand, the last arrival frequently being summoned in the evening to attend an inquisition by the

SCHOOL SLANG

One element of the early O.S. tradition was school jargon. In the *Magazine* of May 1929, an Old Boy reminisced nostalgically about O.S. schoolboy slang: "many of the good old words survive. I am told that any lady, rich or poor, humble or titled is still a 'hag', and any man who is not a 'sahib', a 'Brummer'." 'Hag' is how Kevin FitzGerald referred to the Matron in his youthful reminiscences quoted in Chapter Four. 'Brummer' betrays the School's Birmingham origins. Such terms give a glimpse into the social attitudes of the boys.

An article on 'O.S. Philology' in the *Magazine* of June 1934, reads: "'Big' and 'Young' have nowadays been changed into the uninspired 'one' and 'two' – i.e. 'Big Smith' has become 'Smith one', 'Young Smith' 'Smith two'." The practice of numbering boys with the same surname ceased in 1991 as it threw up too many anomalies. The article omitted the term 'brat' for a junior boy, but included 'soak' [lie-in]; these terms have disappeared during the Woodcote era, as the aspects of school life to which they referred died out.

The article concentrated on uncomplimentary terms for school food and ended with references to language that echoes the public school attitudes of the inter-war years. "'Pater' and 'Mater' of course, remain, in common with most schools, and also that strange Latin word 'Sater'; but in my day one used not to hear 'Frater'."

The Catholic emphasis of the School is reflected in the inclusion in the article of "'Scrapes' [Confession] is still 'scrapes'; 'jaw' [homily from someone in authority} is still 'jaw', though 'pijaw' is rare."

On the other hand the liberal atmosphere suited others. Peter Higgins, a great friend of the famous cookery writer Elizabeth David, was one boy who took advantage of the liberal atmosphere. Through family connections he hunted locally and on OTC. Field Days would borrow a horse and offer himself to the Commanding Officer as a mounted orderly and messenger to avoid a long marching day. Trips to the White Hart at Sonning were also a favourite, if illegal, pleasure. Reading itself was out of bounds but that did not prevent boys from illicitly sampling its attractions.

One incident that epitomised the somewhat cavalier and 'country club' atmosphere of the school in the 1920s was when an Old Boy, Charles Lumsden, flew an aeroplane over the School. Hubert Barry recalled the incident and the excitement it created:

> *"We were in our groundfloor classroom, facing the South front, when suddenly we heard a mighty roar and the next moment an aeroplane flew past the window at nought feet. Needless to say, the classroom, in fact all classrooms, emptied in a flash, with the masters powerless to stop it, and the whole school assembled on the North front where we were treated to a dazzling display of aerobatics. It turned out to be an old boy … who adopted this novel way of visiting his* Alma Mater. *He was flying a Gloster Grebe."*

Prefects. It was a help if you had an older boy as a protector or were promising at sport.

The academic standard was "pretty low" in the words of one Old Boy of the era. The teaching staff was considered, with the notable exceptions of Oliver Welch and Gerald Headlam, as "a mixed bunch". Towards the end of the decade some boys were withdrawn or transferred to other Catholic public schools as a result of the low academic standards and poor results in public examinations.

E.P.'s departure left a major gap. He was succeeded in January 1930 by Father Henry Tristram, in what was, in retrospect, a caretaker capacity. There was no clear-cut successor to E.P. waiting in the wings as there had been in 1872 and 1911. Father Henry had stood in during E.P.'s illness and had not been a success. If Father Sebastian Ritchie was considered at all for the post he was evidently thought to be occupied with the newly-founded preparatory school at Rose Hill. It was clearly the moment for a radical reappraisal of the School's position and future. In the meantime new arrangements for running the School detached from the Birmingham Oratory were being worked out. E.P. loved The Oratory School and did all he could to foster its progress, giving some £40,000 of his own money to it over the years which was a sizeable sum for the time.

At the Prize Giving in 1930 it was recorded in the *Magazine*:

> *"Two presentations were … made to the late Headmaster, Father Edward Pereira, in recognition of the splendid services he has rendered to the school during his long term of office. Lord Fitzalan [sic], on behalf of the Old Boys, presented him with a portrait of himself, brilliantly executed by Simon Elwes, which Father Edward has very generously given to the School. M.F. Callaghan [the School Captain] then presented him with a portable altar on behalf of the present members of the School."*

In September 1930, Richard Hope joined the staff, together with Brother Jocelyn Trappes-Lomax, who taught Mathematics and was to be Second Master from 1931 to 1933, and N. O. Rees. Richard Hope was to play an important role in the School in the coming decade.

Art was taught at Caversham from the first days of the School's move there by Mr Williams, who died of blood poisoning at the end of September, 1924. He was succeeded by Mark Symons, about whom *The Times* posthumously wrote that "he was a very sound craftsman, and, when he was not burdened with a mission, he had a remarkable power of co-ordinating detail painted in a Pre-Raphaelite manner".

Another person who taught Art at Caversham was the later Sir Stanley Spencer. John Ward recalled him: "He held his art class in a small class room just in the arch leading to the old stable block at Caversham [Park]. He was a very pleasant man … [His] efforts to turn me into

an artist were a total failure." When Francis Bird asked Stanley Spencer to sign his autograph book, the artist obliged with a pencil sketch of its owner.

Apart from the games, the principal school activity was the OTC to which all the boys belonged and on which much emphasis was placed. There was also drama, as for example the musical comedies jointly written by Gerald Headlam and St. John Brougham. There was a Debating Society in the 1920s in which members of staff took part, but it lapsed for two or three years around the end of the decade. There was little music of note apart from the Chapel Choir. One of the first acts carried out by Richard Hope on joining the staff in the Michaelmas term of 1930 was to found a Musical Society. Denis Gibson summarised the atmosphere in the School at his time as: "we were frightful snobs; we were tough; we were Philistine …"

The resignation of Father Edward at the end of 1929 and the succession of Father Henry to the headship at the beginning of 1930 were greeted in the *Magazine* with an optimism that did its best to cover inevitable anxiety about the future. Father Henry was to remain

Above: Father Henry Tristram painted by Harold Yates, a drawing master at the School. Father Tristram was Head Master briefly from 1930–1 but served the School for many years in different roles.

Below: Stanley Spencer taught Art at the School in the 1920s.

Below: Stanley Spencer taught Art at the School in the 1920s.

Head Master for five terms, ably supported by Gerald Headlam. The story is that when a Prefect sent a boy to the Head Master the boy replied, "Which Head Master?" However, Father Henry was capable of firm, if dramatic, action. During his period in office he dismissed four members of staff over a disagreement.

At the end of that period in September, 1931 a new regime for control of the School took over from the Fathers of the Birmingham Oratory. The *Magazine* of November, 1931 summarised the new arrangements:

"Another very important step was the formation of a Governing Body … Viscount FitzAlan of Derwent, K.G., was elected Chairman. The Body consists of four representatives from the Birmingham Oratory; three representatives from the Oratory School Society; two from the London Oratory; one representative of the Catholic body at the Universities of Oxford and Cambridge; one member representing His Grace the Archbishop of Birmingham; and finally four co-opted members."

Father Henry Tristram stepped down as Head Master and assumed the title of Warden. Father Edward became the Chaplain. The post of Warden was originally created in order to give a presence in the School to a member of the Birmingham Oratory community, which was still technically responsible for the School since it provided the Trustees. When the Birmingham Oratorians relinquished their connection with the School the office of Warden continued to exist in an honorary capacity and is still granted to someone who has contributed distinguished service to the School such as a retired Head Master.

The new Governing Body then had to appoint a successor to Father Henry. Their choice fell on Father Guy Wyndham Sich, who was supposedly brought to the attention of the Governors by Monsignor Ronald

Below: The announcement of Father Sich's appointment in The Universe.

Knox (the Oxford Governor). He was tall and had a *curriculum vitae* that recommended him to those seeking someone to lead a school for Catholic gentlemen. Sich's education had been at Winchester and Magdalen College, Oxford, where he had become a Catholic. On leaving school he had become an officer in the Grenadier Guards during the First World War and had been severely wounded in April 1918. He had been ordained priest in the Archdiocese of Westminster in 1927, having studied at St Edmund's College, Ware, and in Rome. As Denis Gibson recalled the reaction among the boys to his appointment was: "[one] of relief that somebody had been found for the job who was relatively young … and apparently a gentleman."

CHAPTER SIX

DRIFT TOWARDS CRISIS

Late Caversham, Father Guy Sich and the Honourable Richard Hope, 1931–38

"I hope and believe that boys educated here will always reflect some measure of that quiet unostentatious manner and grasp of the true values of life which were shown to such a high degree by our founder – Cardinal Newman."

– The Hon. Richard Hope in his Prize Day Address as Head Master, 1937

Opposite: A meet of the local foxhounds in front of the North Front of Caversham Park in the 1930s.

It was soon evident after his appointment that Father Sich was not going to suit as Head Master. The boys found unsettling his tendency to bare his soul emotionally in his addresses to the School. He failed to adapt to the temper and expectations of the institution of which he was in charge. Denis Gibson recalled one example of this during Father Sich's address to the School one Sunday evening at Benediction:

> *"Unfortunately I can recall nothing of the bulk of his talk; but it must have been about sex and the inevitable temptations we should all experience. His face was working rather a lot; he became very emotional, and then said something like: 'Of course I have had much temptation and have not always found it easy to beat' or words to that effect, by which time he was almost sobbing and in tears."*

The boys did not realise how badly he had been affected by his experiences during the First World War. Indeed, when later he had returned to parish work in the Archdiocese of Westminster during the Second World War he was again seriously traumatised while in the act

of rescuing the Blessed Sacrament from the tabernacle during an air raid on his church, Our Lady of Victories in Kensington. It was while he was away from the parish convalescing from the effects of the attack that he met the lady whom he was later to marry after he had unilaterally laicised himself. He was excommunicated for this act but the excommunication was subsequently withdrawn through the good offices of Archbishop David Mathew who was later to become a Governor of the School.

Denis Gibson commented on Father Sich's address in retrospect:

> *"Now that we know his eventual fate it is easier to sympathise with him, and commend him for his humility; but I am afraid our general reaction at the time was one of indignation that a man supposed to be our Headmaster could behave thus in our presence. Any such behaviour from EP would have been unthinkable. I do not think that anyone of us who had known EP was other than scandalised. Maybe he was unlucky to follow so soon after the great man."*

A further example of Father Sich's uncertain stability occurred once again in the Chapel on the Feast of Corpus Christi:

"We had an unusual custom at Caversham, which must have been approved by EP as I had seen it take place in his presence. On the feast of Corpus Christi at the main [sung] Mass, just before the consecration a small Guard of Honour consisting of the O.C. of the OTC, with sword at the carry, and 4 senior boys with fixed bayonets, rifles at the slope, would march into the Chapel and halt at the Altar rails. At the elevation they would present arms in a Royal Salute, and when it was over they would about turn and march out again …

"I and all my contemporaries were proud of what was looked upon as something unique to the O.S., and a very special way of asking a blessing on the OTC. I do not think it had ever entered any of our heads that it might be objectionable.

"Unfortunately this is exactly what it turned out to be. It may well be that Fr Sich had not been briefed on what was to take place, but as the order to present arms was being given he turned round, with his face working, and told them to stop. I cannot remember his exact words, but it was something like: 'Stop this – I cannot have this – please go away.' So they did."

Soon after Father Sich's ill-received address in the Chapel, a deputation of senior boys supposedly went to consult Father John Talbot of the London Oratory, who was a regular visitor at Caversham as Extraordinary Confessor and a Governor of the School. Eventually at the end of 1933 Father Sich was recalled to the Archdiocese of Westminster. This left the problem of who should succeed to the headmastership. A brief announcement in the December *Universe* of that year gave the answer:

"The Rev. Guy Windham Sich, M.A., having been recalled to the Archdiocese of Westminster by His Eminence Cardinal Bourne, the Hon. Richard Hope, M.A., will take over the duties of head master of the Oratory School, Caversham, pending a final appointment to the post. The Warden will be the Rev. Edward Pereira and the Chaplain the Rev. Henry Tristram."

In 1934 E.P. was forced by ill-health to retire to Birmingham. The Governors' choice as the new Head Master therefore fell on the current Second Master, Richard Hope. In doing so they gave to the O.S. its first lay Head Master. Indeed he was the first lay Head Master of any Catholic college. They must have hoped that

Below: OTC camp.

Right: Gerald Headlam in command.

Below: A cartoon from the school magazine illustrating the General Inspection. The 'Flying Bedstead' (see box over page) features prominently and Bertie, a small white dog makes an appearance (he can also be seen in the picture on page 84).

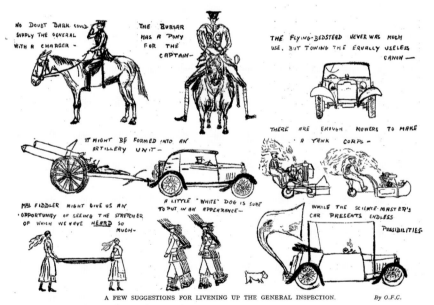

A FEW SUGGESTIONS FOR LIVENING UP THE GENERAL INSPECTION. *By O.F.C.*

a predicament and Hope, immersed as he was in the tradition of the O.S., must have seemed acceptable to them in the circumstances. However the problems that faced him were mounting and the 1930s was not a period favourable to public schools in general. The O.S. as a small school lacking any endowment and without a religious community to support it, was vulnerable to the economic pressures of the age.

In 1932 Father Sich appointed Ronald Richings as Senior English Master who engrossed himself thoroughly in the life of the School for the remainder of the decade. Father George Tomlinson (Head Master 1943–53) wrote of his former colleague on his death in 1962:

"His teaching ability, developed standard of criticism and austere taste in literature, sometimes bordering on the fastidious, won respect for him in class, and outside it his youthful good looks and charm of manner gained him great popularity with masters and boys alike. There used to be repeated the story of how a parent finding him watching a cricket match at Caversham asked whether he was in the 2nd XI yet."

One Old Oratorian from this period, Sir James Comyn, took like a duck to water to the free and easy ways of the School. It says much for his contemporaries that in spite of the disdain of many of them for academic work and

through his knowledge of the School from his O.S. pedigree as a former pupil and a descendant of James Hope-Scott, one of the moving spirits in its foundation, he would bring stability and understanding to the situation caused by the departure of Father Sich from the headmastership.

Hope was a civilised, shy and retiring person by nature who did not leave a vivid memory of himself on the minds of those in the School under him. However after the departure of Father Sich the Governors were in their keenness for organised games they nonetheless respected this Irishman and his intellectual prowess. Perhaps the secret of the respect he gained from his contemporaries lay in the fact that he was not averse to joining in some of the escapades and illegal activities of his era. Here he recounts an illicit expedition to Queen Anne's School, Caversham on November 5th:

"Seven of us went down to Queen Anne's with a variety of fireworks, and lined up at the edge of the playing field, faced in the direction of the main building and what we thought to be the dormitories. We let off our first cascade. Whereupon large and threatening men emerged from the darkness of Queen Anne's and ran towards us. We took to our heels. I ran across the middle of the playing fields in the general direction of the Oratory with all my might. I heard, or thought I heard, the padding of heavy feet behind me. Suddenly I was felled … As I suddenly came to, I found that in fact I had run full tilt into a hockey net and had become enmeshed in it. Happily there was no assailant, no pursuer, no sight or sound. Gathering myself and my senses together, I slowly made my way back to the Oratory, where I was happy to find my companions of the evening all tucked up in their dormitories."

The sequel to this escapade throws interesting light on Richard Hope as Head Master:

"The next morning the headmaster, then the Hon. Richard Hope (as yet unmarried to the matron) sent for nine of us; the culprit seven – and two others who were, on this occasion, completely innocent. It appeared that intelligence between Queen Anne's and the Oratory must have been quite exceptionally good. It had identified the firework 'raiders' as Oratory boys (not too difficult, I suppose) but had got all seven culprits.

"I was unfortunately at the end of the left side of the circle which formed before the headmaster in his study – and he started on the left.

'Did you, Comyn', he asked 'participate' (I never cared for pompous words) 'in a so-called humorous escapade at St Anne's School [sic] last night?' 'Yes, headmaster, I did.'

"He knew better than to ask if I would disclose the names of the others. He asked the others instead. All admitted – except the two who were

Left: Ronald Richings with pupils, 1939.

THE CAVERSHAM CARS

Left: The 'fleet': Thunderbolt, Blackbird, Bluebird and The Bedstead.

Below: Tim Heffernan driving Bluebird, with Gerald Shepherd in front

The story of the Caversham cars begins after the Lord's match of 1933. Senior boys were allowed to remain in London afterwards for the week-end. The Lower School had to be back at Caversham after the game. One senior boy, Rowland Egerton, arranged to meet two of the Lower School in Piccadilly after going to a nightclub, rather than go back to Reading by train. To meet him the Juniors had, without his permission, borrowed the car of James Underhill, the Housemaster of Faber House. On the way back from London, the big end went on the Great West Road. Rowland later wrote: "There was a terrible clanking sound; how we got the car back to Caversham I don't know." James Underhill was naturally not happy. He punished the miscreants and the matter was smoothed over. The car was left abandoned by the garages near the theatre.

Mortimer 'Tim' Wakefield-Heffernan was part of a group of junior boys who assisted James Underhill with the stage lighting. James was the producer of the school plays and the group were well-known in the school for their technical expertise and ingenuity. Tim recalled later that "one day, at rehearsal ... we tentatively asked [Underhill] if we could mess around with his abandoned car. He gave us an unofficial nod: it was an old 1929 Rover 9 with a very tatty fabric body... Bit by bit we got the car going. [It was named] the Flying Bedstead ... [after] Jimmy Underhill's escapades ..." The Flying Bedstead formed the nucleus of a fleet of cars as "On my 'illegal' trips to Emmer Green to get petrol for the Bedstead ... I found at the garage ... a battered Morris Oxford they had used as a tow car and they were willing (after negotiation) to part with it for £3. This was to be the Bluebird." The growing fleet was later augmented by two more cars 'Thunderbird' and 'Blackbird'.

The fleet was maintained and driven with the help of illustrated booklets from the Shell Oil Company. Favoured boys would be instructed in the fundamentals by the group and then left to their own devices; discretion was stipulated and payment might well take the form of supplies of petrol. The Long Drive and other paths in the extensive grounds afforded suitable stretches for practice. On one such run, Charles Flint, took a bend so fast that he carried away the corner of the wooden mowing shed. The car was undamaged. The shed, however, had to be repaired hurriedly. No one commented. Indeed the authorities tolerated and even took advantage of the activity of the group. They often serviced the vehicles of members of staff and the cars were used on Field Days. Favours performed for Prefects kept the group 'fireproof' to use Tim Heffernan's expression.

innocent. He did not believe them until the rest of us (I think I was the leading advocate) persuaded him to the contrary. We were beaten by the headmaster; beating was rare at the Oratory."

Michael Fitzherbert-Brockholes (O.S. 1933–38, Governor 1962– 98) became close to Richard Hope later on in his school career. He remembered his Head Master in 1987 as a:

"… natural and very skilful games player, especially at squash and tennis, and I very often played the latter with him (since my cricket was less than good) and I much preferred tennis. I seldom managed to get anywhere near beating him, but I certainly enjoyed and benefited from playing against him. He was always very fit and spent a good deal of time going for long walks, especially when he had to give up his climbing."

His memories of Richard Hope continue with mention of the latter's love of classical music: "He was both knowledgeable and appreciative of classical music and enjoyed boys coming and listening to his records … This was something of a rival recital to those given by Bones [G.E. Headlam] in his room on his magnificent gramophone with its enormous horn."

In Snowdonia at the beginning of 1937 Richard Hope was climbing with Mr Peacocke, the Science Master, on the Pen-y-Pass side of Snowdon, when he was hit on the head by a falling stone and suffered a fractured skull. He was as a result absent from his duties for the following Lent term, during which time Father Edward Pereira stood in as Head Master. Hope was able to return for the Summer term. Father Henry Tristram also returned to duties after being absent because of illness.

E.P. wrote in April, 1937 to Raymond Clark, a temporary member of the teaching staff, of this brief experience as acting Head Master: "The luck which I have had in being unexpectedly called back to the old life which I so love, in the evening of my life, has been made all the more enjoyable thanks to the keenness you have shown for the School which I have loved for two and sixty years."

E.P. was the Titular Head Master, but Gerald Headlam was "Head in School – and he was Head", according to Clark. Clark's memory of the school into which he had come as a fill-in during Hope's absence is instructive. He felt that:

"[the] Spirit of The School was excellent. Discipline was easy, I found and the innate idea of fair play was well to the fore. Self discipline was much encouraged and any ill conceived 'deviationism' was speedily and effectively dealt with by Headlam, who believed in the words of Holy Writ, 'Spare the rod & spoil the child'. He was scrupulously fair, I found, and I heard very few grumbles from the junior 'fry'."

Then came a surprising development in Hope's headmastership. Michael Fitzherbert-Brockholes recorded his memory of it:

Above: Richard Hope, Head Master, with Cardinal Hinsley and Lord FitzAlan in 1937.

"I do believe that [Richard Hope] was something of a loner in those days, so it came as something of a surprise when he became engaged to Helen Lambart who had come to the school as Assistant Matron. She and her family were great friends of the Pereiras …

"There is no doubt that getting engaged and married brought about a considerable change in Dick and one which helped him to be more forthcoming in

his approach to people. For someone as shy as he was I am sure this was a considerable achievement. I was tremendously flattered when he asked me if I would be his best man at his wedding …"

The marriage of Hope to the Matron became over the years confused by the rumour-mill with the eventual fate of Father Sich. The event led to a scurrilous and unfounded *canard* which was needlessly repeated by the writer, Evelyn Waugh, in a letter that he wrote to Nancy Mitford in 1949, shortly after he had visited the School at Woodcote to give away the Prizes. His letter reads in part:

Right: Senior boys.

Below: 1st XV Rugby team (1937) captained by Michael Fitzherbert-Brockholes (seated centre).

"… I went on Saturday to the Oratory School to give away the prizes. Sixty years ago it was the leading Catholic public school & everyone like Lords FitzAlan and Rankeillour were there. Now there are 34 [in fact, according to the Governing Body minutes of the time, it was 64] boys in a little Queen Anne house smaller than this [his house, Piers Court]. All because of the disastrous appointment of an Anglo-Catholic parson, convert & sex-maniac, as headmaster some years ago."

To be fair to Evelyn Waugh, he was only repeating a commonly held piece of gossip, albeit one often embellished, about the School.

Michael Fitzherbert-Brockholes judged his Head Master and later friend:

"I do not recall discussing general school policy with Dick at any time, with one exception. This was over the question of school prefects being allowed to beat boys for certain misdemeanours. I had strong views about this and remember telling Dick that it would never be my intention to ask for permission to do this as it was a system I did not

Right: Caversham scenes.

*approve of. He was in full agreement with me, and I
remember wondering why then he had never taken
this step himself and I do not know if the practice
had continued after I left."*

Fitzherbert-Brockholes could have added that it was on
the initiative of Prefects like himself and his successor as
School Captain, Michael Stilwell, that the bullying aura
of the 1930s was curtailed. He later viewed the School
over which Hope had presided and his friend's role in its
history:

*"I am sure Dick was not aware of much that went on
in the school – some of it less than good –
nevertheless there was a good spirit and a strange,
almost self-deluding esprit-de-corps which was used
to cover a multitude of shortcomings and which in
my view were a legacy from the days before Dick
took over the reins.*

*"Whether someone other than Dick could have
pulled the school back I don't know as there were
so many factors militating against this, but whatever
Dick may have done it was in a very low key and he
was doing no more than keeping the ship afloat."*

An example of how Richard Hope attempted to change
the School and bring it up to date is his reorganisation of
the School into a Senior (St Philip's) and Junior (St Mary's)
House. Each Division had its own dormitories, recreation
rooms, libraries and changing rooms. These changes
allowed for an improvement in the standard of the
classrooms, which were re-equipped and refurnished

Richard Hope felt that changes in the School's
teaching and curriculum arrangements were needed. In
1936, he introduced the setting of subjects according to
ability. He also introduced a workroom for
"carpentering and mysterious electrical experiments"
and the History Society and the Scientific Society. In

initiating this reorganisation, he obviously felt that problems of insufficient pastoral care and inadequate academic standards should be addressed by changes to the physical context in which they were meant to operate. The by now traditional house divisions were retained for games purposes

Fitzherbert-Brockholes continued his overview of Richard Hope's headship and the School in general:

> "For those of us who have always believed that there was an important role for the Oratory to play in Catholic education for boys we should be thankful for Dick Hope keeping the ship afloat, for it has meant that after the long and at times painful evolution of the school from those lean years the school has achieved the position it now holds among the best Catholic Public Schools."

The Governors were greatly exercised over the state of the School's finances. Two of these were Maurice Molloy who oversaw the fabric of the building and land matters for the Governors, and the Honourable Richard Preston a successful businessman in mining firms who had been co-opted by the Governors and dealt with their negotiations with Lloyds Bank over the School's overdraft with that bank.

Rumours had been abroad for some time that the School was going to close. Hilaire Belloc referred to them in a letter he wrote from Paris in 1934 to Mrs Reginald Balfour. In it his unhappiness at the departure from Edgbaston can still be seen:

> "… I wonder if the Oratory [School] is going to survive? I hear it is in some danger of diminution and I don't wonder – they have taught so little and have such a long era of shilly-shally. It was a great mistake to leave Birmingham. It was a break with all the traditions and that is fatal to an institution."

The Governors sought ways of publicising the School to generate more applications and hence, more revenue. They also looked for economies at the same time as discussing appropriate ways by which to combat the rumours of the School's impending closure.

A number of priests filled the post of Chaplain in the 1930s. Father Henry Tristram had taken over as Warden when he resigned the headmastership in 1931, Father Edward Pereira had taken on the duties of Chaplain at the same time. When ill-health and the strain of headmastering had forced the withdrawal of Father Guy Sich in 1933, they reversed their roles with Father Henry becoming the Chaplain and Father Edward the Warden.

In 1934 when ill-health forced Father Edward to return to Birmingham, Father Hugh Pope took over the function of Chaplain. He was the son of the much-loved Mathematics master at Edgbaston, Richard Pope, and the nephew of Father Thomas Pope of the Birmingham Oratory. After leaving school he had begun training as a doctor but gave that up to enter the Dominicans. He was a founding member in 1931 of the Governing Body as the Representative of Archbishop Williams of Birmingham.

Left: OTC camp with Captain James Underhill.

While Chaplain he also acted as Sub-Warden. In 1935 he was obliged to give up being the O.S. Chaplain on his election as Prior of the Dominican house at Hawkesyard. Father Cyril Rylance of Downside Abbey replaced him. Then Father Henry acted as Chaplain, but was succeeded on a temporary basis by Father Edward Pereira when the former was absent through illness.

Two years later in 1937 the uncertainty over the post was resolved by the arrival of a new Chaplain Father George Tomlinson, who came from the Archdiocese of Westminster to take up the position. He took to the spirit of the School in large measure and was to have a significant role in its future.

Changes in the personnel around the School continued. There was the retirement in 1937 of the Matron Miss Katherine Gay-Smith, to be replaced by Miss Helen Lambart, soon to marry the Head Master. In 1932 Sergeant-Major Warchus retired. He was replaced by Sergeant-Major Stanbridge of the Coldstream Guards. These two loyal servants of the School were rewarded by the Governors for their contribution to its standing by pensions which were maintained even at the moments of the most extreme financial stringency.

In 1937 together with the Matron the School also lost the services of its Bursar Stephen Harding. He was replaced by James Underhill resuming the post he had held prior to Stephen Harding's arrival. In 1936 David Cecil Fowler Burton had joined the staff as 1st XI cricket coach, later also to be 1st XV coach. The maintenance of a successful image at the annual Lord's

Above: A scene from The Man in the Bowler Hat.

fixture against Beaumont was important to all concerned with the School and D.C.F. Burton (he was invariably referred to by his initials) a former Captain of Yorkshire County Cricket Club, managed to do precisely that with a succession of four wins from 1936 onwards. His great friend, the cricket writer and commentator E.W. ('Jim') Swanton, summed up his friend's contribution to O.S. cricket in his *The Daily Telegraph* column of 3rd July, 1996:

> *"I have had a soft spot for The Oratory School ever since my old friend DCF Burton (Yorkshire captain 1919–1921) coached them to four successive victories over Beaumont at Lord's in the late 1930s despite the place being almost devoid of boys. It seemed an annual miracle."*

The matches of 1940 and 1941 were abandoned because of rain with The Oratory in a winning position.

Jim Swanton attended a lunch at the Army and Navy Club in St James's in October, 1996 to mark the 60th anniversary of D.C.F. Burton's association with the School. It was on this occasion that Jim Swanton accepted the invitation to become the President of the O.S.C.C. When he died in 2000 Sir John Paul Getty agreed to follow him in that office. On the latter's death in 2003 Mike Smith of England and Warwickshire took over this honorary position.

James Underhill's notable contribution to the life of the School in the 1930s, apart from his housemastering,

teaching, command of the OTC and bursarial responsibilities, was his series of dramatic productions. They began in December 1930 and became steadily more celebrated and ambitious. In December 1935 he produced Galsworthy's *Escape*. It was the turn of Noel Coward's *Hay Fever* a year later. The following year (1937) Terence Rattigan's *French Without Tears* was the choice. This was the first amateur performance of the play after its great success on the London stage. Terence Rattigan came to see the production of his play which he enjoyed.

Richard Hope did not fully recover from the effects of his climbing accident in early 1937. In the Summer term of 1938, the staff expressed their view to the Governors that: "Mr Hope would not be able to carry on his duties without a prolonged rest." Father Hugh Pope was the link between the Governors and the staff on this matter. He reported back to the Governors that: "the Masters were unanimous in wishing that Mr Headlam might succeed Mr Hope if the latter retired or was absent and that they considered that Mr Headlam should be definitely appointed to act as Headmaster in such a way that he would not feel that he was merely a stop gap, but that there should be no public announcement at present of a new Headmaster."

So Lord FitzAlan as Chairman wrote to Gerald Headlam in July 1938 to inform him that Richard Hope was to be given "prolonged leave of absence and that you are to be asked to undertake the duties of Head Master". Hope finally tendered his formal resignation of the headmastership in November 1938. So the O.S. welcomed its fifth Head Master within the space of nine years. This, however understandable the reasons for it were, was not a recipe for a stable and prosperous school. However, with the advent of Gerald Headlam to the headmastership, the O.S. had stumbled again on its genius for finding at the correct moment the appropriate person for the task facing it.

CHAPTER SEVEN

SURVIVAL

From Caversham via Downside to Woodcote, Gerald Headlam, 1938–42

"I believe that [The Oratory School] still fulfils the purpose formed for it by Cardinal Newman himself:
'To fit men for this world, while it trains them for the next.'"
– Gerald Headlam's first Prize Day address, 1939

Opposite: Gerald Headlam (left), known as 'Bones', at the Royal Berkshire Regimental Garden Party, 1938.

It was Gerald Headlam's devotion to the School that led him to accept the post of Head Master, and tide the institution over its crisis until better times arrived. He was the right man for the moment. He kept the School's continuity unbroken and gave, with his well-dressed and dignified appearance, the School a sense of normality. One member of the Downside Community at the time, who remembered him from this period recalled him as 'decorous'. This was Dom Adrian Morey (Head Master 1953–67) who was soon to know the O.S. better.

Robert de Burlet, in 1987, recalled Gerald Headlam:

"[He] was a charming and endearing man … Tall and distinguished, he was an archetypal bachelor … [He could] play the piano beautifully and amongst my fondest memories of the O.S. are [sic] of Bones playing the Minute Waltz on his beloved baby grand … It was brave of Bones to take on the Headmastership. It must have seemed a daunting prospect, and Bones was nearly blind. But I shouldn't think he was afraid of anything. He must have known that it would be beyond him to rescue the O.S., but with his faith he
must have known that something would turn up, and indeed it did – Tommy."

David Wilson (Governor 1983–2001) wrote of him in later years:

"'Bones' was one of the most likeable masters of the old school type. I never remember him raising his voice in anger. He was a gentleman in the true sense of the word. [He] wore good tailored suits and I remember always a distinct aroma of eau de cologne … His room, the Headmaster's Study was absolutely typical of this. His pride and joy was his gramophone which stood in the far corner surmounted by the most enormous papier mâché horn."

When Gerald Headlam assumed the headship the country was on the threshold of war. There had been much talk in the local press of the possibility of air raids over Reading. Indeed, a bomb did fall near the open-air swimming pool and fractured it.

From the beginning of the Michaelmas term 1940 the boys were sleeping in the cellars. The fact of the impending departure from Caversham and uncertainty about the future imbued the following academic year with sadness. Robin Slater, who was the last School Captain at Caversham, wrote in 1988 of his final term:

"In some ways, one hoped that the clock would stand still and that the term would never end. Tommy [Father Tomlinson] was a tower of strength and helped to keep up everybody's morale. His soirées after night prayers were always something for the prefects to look forward to and Tommy produced copious amounts of green tea as discussions progressed to a late hour on every conceivable topic … How well I remember the last Corpus Christi High Mass. The Guard of Honour presenting arms in the centre aisle. What a splendid sight it was from the altar steps. I remember wondering though where we would all be for Corpus Christi 1942."

In December 1940 Alexander Baillon replaced Dr Heurtley as the Bursar. He was to prove an invaluable servant of the School in the crisis that lay ahead. His commitment to the School is shown by the fact that he sent his four sons to it. Baillon looked after the contents of Caversham Park, while the School was spending its two terms at Downside.

Miss Gay-Smith also retired fully in 1941. On her retirement as the main School Matron in 1937 she had become the O.P.S. Matron. Another notable retirement at this stage was that of Viscount FitzAlan of Derwent as the Chairman of the Governing Body in 1940. He was replaced by Colonel the Honourable Richard Preston. However, Lord FitzAlan was to resume his former position a year later when the financial crisis broke and the pressure of his business interests with the Rio Tinto Corporation forced Colonel Preston to withdraw. Then, in the words of the *Magazine*: "[fortunately], Lord

FitzAlan has consented to resume his old position as Chairman, and it is to his magnificent courage and devotion to his Old School, and his determination to see it once more established in suitable surroundings, that we are chiefly indebted for our present settlement at Woodcote House."

Above: Father Tomlinson in pensive mood at Caversham. In the far distance Gerald Headlam is watching the game.

Above: Boys were soon writing home about the privations of wartime food rationing.

Above right: By 1940 the School's numbers had dropped to below 50.

Wartime had brought food restrictions to Caversham. Robin Allott wrote home in 1941: "You can't get chocolate any more here … [the] food here is dreadful. I'm feeding myself on some cornflakes which I bought."

The seeds of the financial crisis of 1941 had been sown some years earlier. For the financial year ended on 15th September, 1932, there had been a loss of £2,200. The Governors' minutes had rationalised it: "The loss was mainly due to the general economic depression which made it necessary to allow reduced pensions (fees) in many cases where parents could not possibly pay more and which prevented new applications." For the financial year ended on 15th September, 1935 the loss had nonetheless grown to £3,907/4s/5d. In May, 1939, the bank overdraft stood at £9,905. So the School's finances were in a parlous state by the end of the decade.

Rumours about the School's closure had been current on the Catholic grapevine before the outbreak of the Second World War. In reporting to the Governors on 25th July, 1938, about a Board of Management meeting discussing the financial plight of the School, Lord Rankeillour pointed out:

"[that] the finance available would not under present conditions carry the School on for more than 4 terms ahead and that there were various matters which should be considered as soon as

possible, namely the expediency of taking day boys, the question of the arrangement of a permanent mortgage in discharge, or part discharge of the loan by Lloyds Bank, Birmingham and the question of advertising the School in order to obtain more boys."

The numbers in the School in May 1939 totalled 52 pupils, while there were 25 in the O.P.S. At a meeting of the Governing Body on 26th June, 1939:

"Lord Rankeillour detailed the steps which had been taken to put forward a scheme for the financial assistance of the School under which Old Boys and other friends of the School were to be asked to enter into covenants to contribute annual sums during a period of 7 years in such a way as to effect a saving of income tax, for the benefit of the School, on their contributions."

It ended with the approval of a resolution:

"This meeting is of opinion that the scheme of obtaining covenants laid before it should be proceeded with, but that before the scheme with the covering letter from the Duke of Norfolk is sent round generally endeavours should be made privately to obtain a first list of contributors."

This mention of Duke Bernard's support heralds the latter's willingness over the coming decades to lend to his old School both his financial support as well as the prestige of his presence and name as it struggled to survive and re-establish itself in the post-War world.

By September, 1940 there was a loss of £4,119/0s/1¾d, making a total loss of £30,711/17s/11¾d. This was reported to the Governing Body by the Council of Management in 1942:

"The Council of Management has to report that the Board of Management closed the School at Caversham Park, Reading, after the Summer Term 1941, because the premises were sold by Lloyds Bank Ltd., as Mortgagees under their powers contained in Mortgages and Charges on the premises created by the Trustees for the Congregation of the Oratory at Birmingham, in whom the Caversham Park premises were vested."

Indeed Colonel Preston, the Chairman, wrote to Father Philip Lynch of the Birmingham Oratory (Assistant Head Master 1917–25, Governor 1931–41) in May, 1941, with the view that: "The Oratory School can no longer continue." Preston was equally pessimistic about the prospect of a move of the School's premises. Again he wrote to Father Philip on 5th June, 1941 saying that: "… the chances of carrying on the School elsewhere are so slender as to be disregarded, for practical purposes, as outside the bounds of possibility".

The Chairman said three Governors disagreed with that conclusion. It is reasonable to assume that the identities of these three are the trio mentioned in this context by Father Tomlinson in his Prize Day speech of 1949: FitzAlan, Rankeillour and Dick Dean. Colonel Preston wrote that he would: "have put it to the Governors that the sale of the premises meant the end of the School".

In fact by the end of June 1941 the Chairman had changed his mind in view of the "extraordinary price" obtained for Caversham Park, which was £55,000. The Fathers of the Birmingham Oratory, however, felt that the sale of the School meant the end of its existence and as some of their number included the Trustees they received the money from the purchasers (estimated at between £9,000 and £10,000). Being concerned about their liability and lacking confidence in the administration of the School by the Association during the previous decade they were reluctant to hand over the surplus amount after the clearance of the indebtedness. They were anxious to protect the financial position of the Birmingham Oratory and its various charitable activities in the City of Birmingham.

So the die was cast. It was decided to close the School and to sell off the premises to pay off the overdrafts with the bank. Maurice Molloy was appointed by his fellow Governors as their agent for the sale. Caversham Park was sold to the B.B.C. to become its Monitoring Station which it remains to this day. News of the closure caused bewilderment and dismay among parents of the boys, although the boys themselves were alert to the identity of the purchasers and were resigned to the fact of the School moving. Some boys were transferred to other schools by their parents, but most parents remained loyal to the O.S. Maybe this was because upheaval was a factor of the times and people were prepared to put up with inconvenience because of the War. Many, however, remained loyal because they valued the ethos of the School and wished to see it preserved.

Robin Allott wrote to his parents in July, 1941:

"I'll be glad to go in a way. The O.S. was certainly getting a bit ramshackle and if the Germans bombed Reading heavily, the O.S. would make a lovely target with the moon shining on it. Also the building was becoming more and more a part of Reading. I hope we go somewhere deep in the country. "

Above and right: The School moved to Woodcote House in 1942.

The minute to the Governing Body from the Council of Management confirmed the sale of Caversham and then appealed to the Birmingham Oratory to hand over the surplus from the sale:

> *"to the Association for the purpose of purchasing and capitalising the new School premises which are being re-opened at Woodcote House, Southstoke, Oxford. Meanwhile the school for the Michaelmas and Easter terms has been carried on at Downside Abbey thanks to the kind hospitality of the Father Abbott [sic]."*

This new home was to be Woodcote House, a pleasant but unpretentious Queen Anne house set in beech woods on a summit of the Chiltern Hills, some seven miles north of Reading.

At Downside the O.S. boys were accommodated in their own wing separate from the monastic school. They joined Downside classes and activities. They also played for Downside teams. In an article written for the *Magazine* of August 1942 after the O.S. had settled at Woodcote, Gerald Headlam outlined the arrangements that the O.S. enjoyed from September 1941 to April 1942, during its stay at Downside:

"They placed at our disposal a large dormitory and dayroom, three studies for our prefects and a refectory to enable us to retain our identity on the domestic side, while for school work, military training and games we were to join with Downside. We became, in fact, a separate Oratory house parallel with the four houses into which the School is already divided."

The Caversham staff was dispersed on its closure. However the school clung on to its separate identity, notwithstanding the fact that it had few boys, no staff and no buildings. Closer to complete oblivion it could not have come without entirely disappearing. The Governors, under the determined leadership of FitzAlan, were definite that The Oratory School should retain its independence. When the Abbot of Downside offered the prospect of amalgamation, with The Oratory reduced to the name of a house within Downside, FitzAlan is supposed to have replied with a monosyllabic "nope".

On Prize Day of July, 1949 Father Tomlinson told his audience about this fact:

"… it is certain that had the offer been accepted, the Oratory as we know it would not have been in existence today. That the offer was not accepted, that Woodcote House was bought, that the School was moved here and established in face of war-time difficulties was, in the main, the work of three men, the late Lord FitzAlan, the late Lord Rankeillour and Mr S.R. Dean."

The only staff members to accompany the boys to Downside were the Head Master, Miss E.M. Fox, the Head Master's Secretary, and D.C.F. Burton, the cricket coach. The fact that the latter went to Downside shows the importance given to the Lord's fixture in O.S. circles. Francis Whitlaw mentions this point in his recollections of the arrangements at Downside:

Above: The Oratory School spent two terms at Downside before moving to Woodcote. The boys were accommodated in their own wing but joined the Downside boys for lessons.

Right: The triumvirate who are credited with saving the School during the Second World War:

Lord FitzAlan (O.S. 1865–72) as Chairman of the Board of Governors led the School through its time at Downside and oversaw its safe arrival at Woodcote. FitzAlan House was named in his honour in 1957.

Baron Rankeillour (O.S. 1882–8) took over as Chairman of the Governing Body in 1947 on the death of his uncle, Lord FitzAlan.

Dick Dean (O.S. 1916–18) became a Governor and worked closely with Viscount FitzAlan and Lord Rankeillour. On Lord Rankeillour's death in 1949 he took over as Chairman until 1977, when he became President of the Oratory School Association.

> *"Bones took up residence in a lodge in the village, followed shortly by Mrs Stilwell, our adopted foster mother; they jointly spent their time drying us out after our cider farm outings, keeping the non-conformists under control and liaising with our parents. I remember well on one occasion Bones warning us that his greatest worry was the prospect of being thrown out. His only card was the Lord's match, which he said he would 'never surrender'! However the Community were more than hospitable in accommodating us in the circumstances."*

In this connection, there is a story that Gerald Headlam was approached by Downside offering to be caretakers of the fixture until The Oratory was back on its feet again and in a position to do justice to the prestige fixture. Bones is said to have replied: "There are some 30 boys in this school and I'm reliably informed that only eleven of them are required for a cricket side." Those who knew him find such a reply typical of his dry humour and courage in the situation. Ironically when Beaumont College was closed by the Jesuits in 1966, Downside replaced them as the Oratory's opponents.

In the meantime negotiations continued for the School to take over Woodcote House. The impatience for this to happen was expressed by FitzAlan when he was on a visit to Downside accompanied by Dick Dean. He was heard to remark loudly, oblivious to whoever was listening: "Dean, get us out of here as soon as possible."

Robin Allott, writing to his parents in November, 1941, recorded a visit by FitzAlan to the School in which he referred to the School's new home:

> *"The governors or rather four of them came down and visited the O.S. yesterday, All Saints Day, and Lord FitzAlan said that there was a house in the hills somewhere that wasn't yet for sale but was going to be in a short time and that he Lord F-A didn't want anyone to know that it would be vacant in case the Army took it over. Also he said that he was going to speak to Capt. Margerison [sic] [Captain Margesson was the Secretary of State for War in Churchill's Cabinet at the time], a friend of his, to arrange that the Army shouldn't take it over."*

The embarrassment over the reason why the School had left Caversham Park meant that mention of it by those involved was couched in a range of euphemisms and ambiguities. These gave rise to the belief held for a long time that the School had moved out because the building had been requisitioned. For example, Gerald

Headlam began his article in the *Magazine* of August 1942 about the School's stay at Downside: "Owing to unforeseen difficulties arising from wartime conditions it became necessary at the end of the Summer term 1941 to find a temporary home for the School."

FitzAlan writing a letter published in *The Field* in October, 1942, to announce the School's new home began:

> "Sir, – The Oratory School, late of Caversham Park, which was taken over for other purposes, has now been transferred to Woodcote House, South Oxon, seven miles from Reading. This marks a new development in an old-established Catholic public school. With the fine record of the old boys of service to Church and State, more especially in the Army, the enterprise of the Governing Body, of which I am chairman, in establishing the school in new and beautiful surroundings, deserves every encouragement from the Catholic public, and will no doubt make a strong appeal to the old boys, whose loyalty and devotion to the school have always been so deep and steadfast."

The rumour about the requisition of Caversham Park was convenient as it drew a veil of discretion over the circumstances that had prompted the enforced departure from the grand premises overlooking Reading. Traumatic as that severance had been, it is now regarded as a blessing in disguise. The fabric of Caversham Park was to cost its new owners a large amount to make it watertight in the 1980s, leaving aside the crippling running costs that would have fallen to the School, had it remained there. The design of the building would have meant costly alterations to make it conform to current Health and Safety regulations. The move also permitted the quiet discarding of some ingrained, costly and unnecessary traditions and practices, which would have hindered its

TOMMY AND A PUBLIC SCHOOL HOAX

There has been speculation about the fate of Caversham Park: whether it was requisitioned or sold from economic necessity. The truth behind the sale is gleaned from a 1948 letter written by Father Tomlinson in reply to H. Rochester Sneath, Headmaster of Selhurst School, 'near Petworth, Sussex'. Sneath was in fact a Cambridge undergraduate, Humphry Berkeley, who wrote a series of hoax letters to public figures throughout the late 1940s. Berekeley's letter to Tomlinson began:

Dear Headmaster,
I understand that your School, like mine, had to undergo the trouble of evacuation in the war. I thought, therefore, that you might be interested to know that my Solicitors have discovered that there is a loophole in the existing law that would enable us to claim some quite substantial sums of money from the Government … My Solicitors assure me that though no charge in the Courts could result, the method might perhaps be thought a trifle dishonest. However, it would be in a good cause, and, surely for a Jesuit like yourself, that would be alright!
Yours very truly,
H. Rochester Sneath

Father Tomlinson's reply ran:

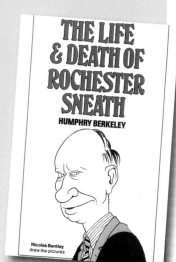

Dear Headmaster,
Very many thanks for your letter of April 22nd. I am interested in what you say of the possibility of making a claim on the Government on account of evacuation of our premises during the war.
I don't know whether it would apply in our case as we decided in the end to sell our former property at Caversham Park outright to the B.B.C. …
I have not the honour to belong to the Jesuits, but I shall none the less be interested to hear any further news on this subject which you may have to impart.
Yours sincerely,
G.A. Tomlinson

progress in the post-War era and the abandonment of which would have caused ructions under less desperate circumstances.

Another person from the School's previous existence who now arrived was Bernard (Barney) Webb. He had been on the staff of the O.S. in its later years at Edgbaston and in the early days at Caversham where he had helped greatly with coaching as the School switched football codes from Association to Rugby. He now rejoined his former colleague Gerald Headlam as

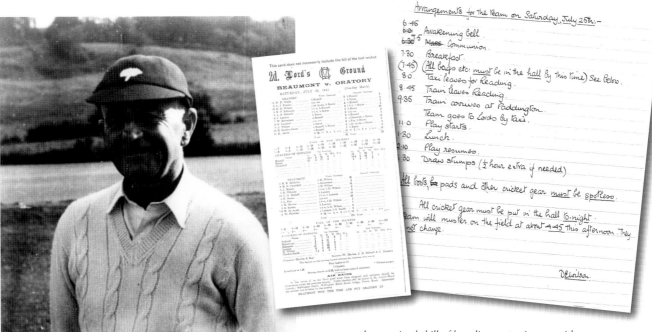

Right: D.C.F. Burton, the inspirational cricket coach and the only member of the teaching staff who accompanied the boys to Downside.

Centre: The Lord's cricket card for 1942 includes instructions on what to do in the event of an Air Raid.

Top right: The Captain of Cricket's handwritten instructions for the boys playing in the Lord's XI in July 1942.

his Second Master. In the interim he had been serving on the staff of Beaumont College. As an experienced schoolmaster who knew the workings of the O.S. he was an invaluable acquisition as the School sought to re-establish itself in its new home.

D.C.F. Burton came back from Downside and now faced the Herculean task of producing a 1st XI to honour the fixture at Lord's, having only a small pool of boys to draw upon and poor facilities for cricket. The School did manage to obtain the use of Huntley & Palmers' ground in Kensington Road, Reading. The Captain of Cricket for the Lord's match, David Wilson, later wrote of the occasion in the *Magazine*:

> *"By 1942 the O.S. had not lost this fixture since 1935 … Play started at Lord's at 11 a.m. Beaumont won the toss and put the O.S. in to bat … By lunchtime at 1.30 p.m. Beaumont had already passed our score [45 all out] … After lunch a sense of desperation was descending and, as a dire measure, I exercised a captain's privilege and put myself on as the fifth change in the bowling. Heavenly assistance arrived rather late, but nonetheless acceptable. By an extraordinary fluke I found I was able to reproduce a*

recently acquired skill of bowling outswingers with an old ball; I still have the small silver mug I was awarded afterwards for my figures of 5 wickets for 20 runs. I have never been able to swing an old ball since. Beaumont were all out for 124. In we went again to bat … and we were all out for 65 … Beaumont had won by an innings and 11 runs.

> *"Dreadful as this all reads, I suppose we could not have expected anything else from such a handful of a school. At least we had fielded a team and perhaps did our bit towards the achievement of O.S. cricketers nowadays and the marvellous grounds on which they play."*

Also returned with the School from Downside was Miss Fox who added to her previous duties and became the Household Manageress. Alexander Baillon remained the Bursar.

With the School settled at Woodcote Gerald Headlam's task was complete. The thread of continuity was unbroken. So it was no surprise when he decided to step down. Robin Allott reported his announcement of his resignation in a letter to his parents in December, 1942:

> *"On Wednesday morning Bones came in as usual to say the prayers before work starts and he told us quite gaily that he was going to retire since he was getting too old and at the same time he announced that Fr. Tomlinson who at present has a parish in London … was going to be the headmaster next term."*

WOODCOTE

The manor of Rollins or Rawlins in the Parish of South Stoke, Oxfordshire, was obtained by the Knapp family at the time of the Dissolution of the Monasteries. A member of the family, Temple Stanyan, built the later Woodcote House in its grounds. This was afterwards inherited by Thomas Fraser who was High Sheriff and Deputy Lieutenant of Oxfordshire. In 1770 he built the room now called the Adam Room, for a visit of George III. Its elaborate plaster ceiling is one of the main features of the House.

The estate was inherited by a female descendant of Thomas Fraser who had married Adam Duff, a grandson of the 1st Earl of Fife. Then the family surname became Fraser Duff. In 1845 Adam "was obliged to let Woodcote, owing to his great generosity to his brothers". An earlier tenant of the house from 1827 to 1829 was the novelist Bulwer Lytton. Then from 1845 it was let to the Reverend Philip Nind, Vicar of South Stoke-cum-Woodcote. He founded a fashionable preparatory school there which was continued by his son the Reverend Hubert Nind, who had succeeded his father in the living of South Stoke, and another headmaster, the Reverend J.H. Wilkinson. Woodcote House was inherited by Robert Fraser Duff, great-nephew of Thomas and his wife Eleanor. Eleanor's sister Laura had married Adam's younger brother Thomas. They were the parents of Thomas Fraser Duff whose son Robert sold the house in 1912 to the Honourable Charles Hanbury-Tracy.

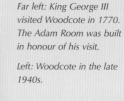

Far left: King George III visited Woodcote in 1770. The Adam Room was built in honour of his visit.

Left: Woodcote in the late 1940s.

Above and above right: The kitchen garden and green house in the early 1900s.

Right: Some of the first boys at Woodcote, 1944.

"It's perfectly lovely here; the walls of the house have wisteria covered with flowers now; virginia creeper and millions of plants I don't know on them. The building itself is Queen Anne style … and inside a lot of panelling … I'm writing this letter in a room called the Black Room, rather like the library of the O.S., if you can remember it. In the garden are a profusion of flowers and flowering bushes, lovely rhododendrons, wonderful azaleas and multi-coloured lilacs. The kitchen garden is terribly well-kept … Food here is quite good but cook crises are quite frequent. The main difficulty about this place is its inaccessibility …"

It was at this point that the well-known architect, Detmar Blow, remodelled the house. He made the original front hall an imposing barrel vaulted chamber with a white ceiling and a gold frieze of acanthus leaves. Its gold picks up on the gold which frames the striking black panels of the walls. To obtain the necessary dimensions for his room, he raised the original ceiling into the floor above inserting *oeil de boeuf* windows at the top of the room. The original saloon to which the hall led was turned into an entrance hall with a black and white marble floor. A new front door was inserted into this new entrance hall with an elaborate shell-like canopy above it.

Woodcote House was converted into a hospital during the First World War by Mrs Hanbury-Tracy. Her husband, who was to succeed to the title of Lord Sudeley of Toddington, sold the house to the Honourable Algernon Borthwick and it became his family's home until they decided to sell it after his death in 1941.

This was the house to which Gerald Headlam came with some 30 boys, to re-open the School on 6th May, 1942. Robin Allott's communication to his parents, written after a fortnight at Woodcote, was full of his new impressions, as the O.S. struggled to find its way in the fourth home of its existence:

CHAPTER EIGHT

BACK FROM THE BRINK

Early Woodcote, Father George Tomlinson, 1943–53

"The young man Cardinal Newman trained through the Oratory School was first of all a Catholic and a devout one, secondly, he was a man who loved knowledge not for the sake of what it enabled him to do or be, but for its own sake, and thirdly, he was a young man who found the deep spring of his own attitude and actions in himself rather than in the words of others."

– Father Tomlinson speaking on Prize Day, 1949

Opposite: The portrait of Father George Tomlinson by John Redvers, which hangs in the Tomlinson Arts Centre.

Below: Some of the first boys at Woodcote.

The O.S. did not have the most auspicious of beginnings in its new home at Woodcote. The Fathers of the Birmingham Oratory had retained the money received from the sale by the Trustees, who were members of the Community. They did so because they were uncertain about the School's prospects, especially as they had been unhappy about the Governors'

direction of it over the previous decade. The latter now required the remaining balance of that sum after the settlement of the Caversham Park indebtedness to purchase the School's new premises.

The heirs of Algernon Borthwick had sold Woodcote House to the Association for £14,000. It must have weighed with them in concluding the deal that thanks to FitzAlan's influence the house would not be taken over by the Army. This had been the ruin of many houses of similar size during the wartime emergency and must have seemed a particularly likely fate given that there was military activity in the beech woods all around.

Henry Stilwell recalled the wartime activity in the vicinity:

"Prior to the 1944 invasion of occupied Europe, American troops began to arrive in increasing numbers and a large camp was set up in the woods beyond Checkendon to house some of their units. The first time some Americans appeared for Mass in our Chapel they expressed amazement at the absence of girls in the school. Their experience was of course of an entirely co-educational system."

Right: The B.B.C.'s Monitoring station located at Caversham Park, the School's previous home, was fully operational during the Second World War. The School Library (opposite) transformed into the B.B.C.'s main listening room.

Below right: A Lancaster bomber. The boys at Woodcote heard Allied bombers flying overhead on their way to raid German targets.

Nevertheless the conflict did bring its reminders to the boys in the quiet of South Oxfordshire, according to Henry Stilwell:

"In our quiet corner of the world we were nevertheless very aware of the war. Sometimes at night one could see the glow of fires in London and flares dropped by the German bombers. In bed one would hear hundreds of RAF bombers roaring overhead on their way to Germany and returning at dawn."

The tale of the dispute with the Birmingham Oratory over the release of the proceeds of the sale of Caversham Park can be continued in the words of a report written about the circumstances for the Governing Body by Veale Wasbrough, solicitors to the Oratory School Association:

"Feelings ran high and were reflected in public statements on both sides … [opinion] differed within the Birmingham Oratory regarding the disposal of the surplus from the sale of Caversham Park, but the broad view was that the Association's administration of the School during the 1930's had been marked by serious mismanagement and there was a total lack of confidence in the Governing Body."

The extent of the disagreement between the Association and the Community at Birmingham was illustrated by the Birmingham Fathers' concern over the continuing use of the name 'Oratory' attached to any relocation of the School even though they indicated a willingness to accept arbitration on the destination of the funds from the sale of Caversham Park to the B.B.C. The Fathers had consistently argued that The Oratory School had ceased to exist with the sale of Caversham Park.

In addition the Community was unwilling to risk being associated for a second time with an institution

which it felt was likely to fail financially and there was a proper concern on the part of the Trustees that a surplus from the sale of Caversham Park should be dealt with in a prudent way. For this latter reason it was important for the Community that any agreed settlement with the Association was endorsed by the Courts. This lack of confidence on the part of the Birmingham Fathers was given clear expression when in October, 1941 four members of the Governing Body and representatives of the Birmingham Oratory, resigned. The dispute eventually went to court and the case was heard in Chambers by Mr Justice Roxburgh who delivered judgment in February, 1946 endorsing the settlement reached between the Fathers and the Association.

Below: The Library during the Second World War.

The core of that Settlement was a compromise on the disputed Rose Hill loans whereby the Association agreed a payment of £1,800 to the Community in complete discharge of the counterclaims of both parties over the sums mutually owing to them in connection with the former home of the Oratory Preparatory School in Emmer Green near Caversham Park. The pensions of former employees were secured and the balance of the Caversham sale proceeds which in December, 1945, amounted to £14,658/10s/9d, was paid to the Association. A bank loan of £5,500 on the security of the Duke of Norfolk and of Lord Rankeillour had enabled the Association to discharge the balance of the purchase money owing on Woodcote House, the remaining £7,500 being left on a ten-year mortgage by the Borthwick family. Following the settlement, this loan on the security of these two generous benefactors could now be repaid, leaving a small balance to boost the working capital of the School.

Thus an unhappy chapter in the relationship between the Birmingham Community and the Association was finally brought to a close. Of more immediate importance was the lifting of the financial uncertainty which had overshadowed the School and hampered Father Tomlinson's efforts to rebuild it.

Father Tomlinson's aims were to make sure that the Newman pedigree was fused with awareness of the new home and that the old pride in the School which he had experienced and been captivated by as the Chaplain at Caversham should be transferred to Woodcote. The Governing Body complemented his policy of trying to graft onto the School's new location the pedigree and reputation of The Oratory School of earlier years by appointing in November 1945, eminent Old Oratorians to their number. These included the Duke of Norfolk and Lieutenant-General Sir Adrian Carton de Wiart V.C.

In the meantime Father Tomlinson had already set about his self-appointed ends. He should in all justice be credited with restoring the School's belief in itself after the trauma of the double move. His successor, Dom Adrian Morey, who built much of the existing campus and got the outside world to believe in the School's viability, once commented with profound respect that: "I could not have done what Father Tomlinson did." Between them they laid the foundations of the modern-day school. The former provided the dream, the latter gave it practical reality.

A pressing need for Father Tomlinson was to increase the number of boys. He went about this task with a painstaking care, which was reinforced by his personal charm. Bob Symington wrote in 1998 of Tommy:

"Looking back I think his outstanding achievement was in giving the 30 or so boys in the school … a real sense of pride in the O.S. and themselves, and the acceptance that it was quite normal for a public school to have only 30 pupils."

Dr Henry Will was one of the group that came to the O.S. in September 1944 and later recalled the circumstances:

"I first met Tommy in 1944 when he visited my prep school, Wellbury Park. To the surprise of my Headmaster, not to say his disapproval, my parents had chosen to send me to the OS in preference to Ampleforth. That parents such as mine, with no connections with the school, should have selected the OS in preference to better-known and established schools was due, I believe, in no small measure to the favourable impression which Tommy made on them … His ability, against this unpromising background to win the confidence of parents who had no OS connections was a crucial factor in the survival of the School."

Dr Will later became a moving light as its Chairman in the Monsignor Tomlinson Memorial Appeal dedicated to

raising money for a range of causes dear to Monsignor Tomlinson's heart. When the Appeal's Committee decided in 2005 that it had progressed as far as it reasonably could, it decided to transfer the Appeal's capital to the School to help to fund the new Tomlinson Building Art Centre which was opened by Dr Will on 7th June, 2008.

The former squash court had had to be converted into a temporary chapel in 1943, because on 17th October in that year the Chapel caught fire. Such an event might have been seen as a setback to the struggling school but it was not subsequently viewed as such. Although accounts of this fire may vary all agree on one hazard that was posed by it in that, as Henry Stilwell later wrote:

"[the] cadet force armoury, which was over the sacristy, was well ablaze and the ammunition began to blow up in rapid succession. Under this hail of bullets the fire brigade beat a hasty retreat. Their anxieties were increased when an aircraft was heard approaching and it was feared it might be a German bomber attracted by the blaze."

Above: The opening of the Tomlinson Building Art Centre, 2008. On the left is Mr Michael Hasslacher, Chairman of the Governing Body and a member of a family with a connection to the School going back to before the First World War. To the right is Dr Henry Will, Chairman of the Tomlinson Memorial Trust, which funded the new Art Centre named after his Head Master.

THE CRICKET FIELD PROPOSED
AT THE ORATORY SCHOOL
G A TOMLINSON
27TH MARCH 1945

Right: An artist's impression of the Cricket field, 1945. It was drawn by Father Tomlinson, who was a talented amateur artist.

Below: The Cricket field was constructed after the Second World War to commemorate the Oratorians who gave their lives in the War.

Father Tomlinson's Prize Day speech of July 1945 recorded a steady rise in numbers in the School:

"I remember a conversation I had with Lord FitzAlan in 1943 when I was appointed Headmaster, when I said that my first aim would be to raise our numbers to 60, and after that we should have to build. I am hoping in the course of the next week or two to be able to write to our Chairman to say that I have fulfilled my promise."

By the spring of 1946 work was in progress on what has become a striking feature of the Woodcote campus. In his Prize Day speech of 1946 Father Tomlinson stated:

"[hitherto] we have been at a great disadvantage in not possessing a ground large enough for cricket. It has been decided by the Governing Body that our War Memorial, to some forty old boys who lost their lives in the war, should take the form of the provision of such a field. The progress of the work speaks for itself, and I hope that we shall have a really first-class ground next season. "

In fact, there are the names of 45 Old Oratorians commemorated on the World War Two memorials in the Chapel. This compares with the 87 Old Boys who gave their lives in World War One and whose names are again preserved on the memorials in the Chapel. The construction of this field as a War Memorial exemplifies the confidence in the School's survival that existed at this difficult stage.

In the meantime extra teaching space for the expanding numbers was provided in September 1946 by a temporary classroom in the garden, to be followed two terms later by a second one next to it.

In March, 1949 Father Tomlinson wrote a revealing letter to Major George Anne which underlines the sizeable task he had of connecting the older generation of Old Boys with the new home of the School. This task was obviously made easier in the case of the Old Boys of the Edgbaston era since the School they had known had already moved once before from the premises they had known as boys:

> "The school is recovering little by little the fame it once had, and though a great deal remains to be done I feel that the future cannot be as difficult as the past six years have been. We are now 70 strong here and have a Preparatory School near Bournemouth of 80; in 1943 there were 25 boys at the Oratory and no Preparatory School at all, and everything seemed despairing and hopeless. Fortunately the old traditions proved capable of revival and to-day it feels like a School, the School, again."

The successful beginning of Father Tomlinson's task of reviving the O.S. is shown in the comments made by Denis Gibson about Woodcote in 1952 on a later visit to the School:

> "Things were still pretty primitive, but at least there was promise of better things to come and I became very enthusiastic about the long-term possibilities. There was an atmosphere of old times, and I remember feeling very happy that the O.S. had come home at last."

So at the beginning of the 1950s there were signs apparent that 'Tommy', as he was usually and affectionately termed, had managed to achieve his aim of beginning the restoration of the O.S. to its old pedigree and status. He sought every opportunity of

Left: The Second World War memorial in the Chapel.

Below: Distinguished Prize Day speakers included Douglas Woodruff (left) and Evelyn Waugh (right).

Above: Old Boys' Dinner, 1948. Standing behind the top table (fourth from the right) is Gerald Headlam. To his immediate right is Dick Dean and one place beyond him is Father Tomlinson. The revival of the Old Boys' Dinner marked a significant step in the recovery of the School after the move from Caversham to Woodcote.

doing this, for example by inviting high-profile personalities to preside on Prize Day, such as Douglas Woodruff, Editor of *The Tablet* in 1943, the Duke of Norfolk in 1945 and Lieutenant-General Walter Lentaigne in 1946. Evelyn Waugh was the Prize Giver in 1949 and in 1952 the Earl of Lytton came to perform that task, accompanied by the Countess.

Father Tomlinson made the commemoration of Newman's conversion an annual event. He then progressively set about reviving traditional school events which had lapsed. In 1945 the athletic sports were put on again. The school cross country was also revived. The *Magazine* recorded these revivals, the *Magazine* itself representing a survival and continuation of an old O.S. institution, dating back to 1891.

Drama made its appearance once more in the O.S. with a Sixth Form performance in 1945 of Lord Dunsany's *A Night at an Inn*. This had been put on last in 1926. In 1948, the tradition of the Christmas play was brought back with a performance of Shakespeare's *Twelfth Night*, to be followed the next year by *Richard II*.

Sporting encounters with Old Oratorian teams were also re-established, as was the Old Boys' Dinner.

The post of Chaplain under Father Tomlinson was filled by a range of priests in the early years. Father Tomlinson himself had been a popular Chaplain during his time in that post at Caversham. He had a great love of the Church, of the Oratorian spirit of St Philip Neri and of the sacred liturgy which he made as grand as the restricted circumstances at Woodcote allowed.

When Father Coombe, who had taken over as temporary Chaplain in May 1942, was recalled to the diocese of Southwark that year he was replaced by Father Percy Clune. Father Clune left in July 1943 to become Parish Priest of Peterborough and was succeeded by Father Walter Edwardes, the brother of Major David Edwardes. Father Edwardes was forced by ill-health to retire in July 1946 and the post was filled on a temporary basis by Father Edmund Rees-Jones until the arrival of Father Harding in October 1946. The next Chaplain was Father Martin Hughes, a Capuchin. When he was recalled by his Order in 1949, he was succeeded by Doctor Albert Knight until Dom Hubert van Zeller came from Downside to fill the position in which in 1951 he was succeeded by his fellow Downside monk Dom Adrian Morey. Downside therefore continued to be a source of support and encouragement to the School as it struggled to re-establish itself on the Woodcote campus.

An important aspect of Father Tomlinson's task of rebuilding the School was to gather together an effective teaching staff. He had been given an ideal cornerstone with his predecessor's appointment of Barney Webb as Second Master when the School moved into Woodcote House. He was an efficient teacher for examinations and a firm disciplinarian.

In the background was the discreet and loyal presence of Gerald Headlam. On stepping down from the headship, now that his task of bringing the remnants of the O.S. back intact from Downside and of settling them into Woodcote House was complete, he withdrew to the panelled room upstairs with the honorary title of Dean to resume his previous role as the School's 'Mr Chips'.

Father Tomlinson appointed members of staff who he knew would be as committed as himself to the ideal of the School and the restoration of its former glory. In 1947, Michael Tolkien, the second son of Professor J.R.R. Tolkien, came from the Dragon School in Oxford.

In need of a Mathematics teacher, Father Tomlinson asked Professor T. Sulimirski, Director of a refresher course for expatriate Poles at London University, whether he could recommend anyone for the post. The Professor's son Witold (O.S. 1947–51) was then a boy at The Oratory. His recommendation led to the arrival of Stefan Zwierzynski who joined the staff in May 1949 to become one of the legendary characters of the O.S. at Woodcote. 'Zulu' as he was affectionately nicknamed by the boys unable to get their tongues around his surname, brought rigour and discipline to his teaching of Maths and a conscious professionalism to his conduct of his classes.

J.R.R. TOLKIEN

Michael Tolkien (OS 1934–9) joined the staff in 1947. He lived in Chapel Cottage and during the Summer of 1949 his parents stayed to take advantage of the quiet, out-of-term campus and allow J.R.R. Tolkien to work on *The Lord of the Rings*.

Tolkien, in his later role as Assistant Secretary of the Oratory School Society, represented a link with the Old Boys. He also began the task of sorting out the School's records, which led eventually to the setting up of the School's Archives, and to the first post-war edition of the Yellow Book, a comprehensive list of all Old Boys with their addresses.

Dr Will recalled the arrival of the new Games Master at the School, later his friend, Mario Binyon:

"Into this rumbustious and slightly dysfunctional world Mario Binyon parachuted as Games Master in 1946. To us boys he seemed invariably genial, a man of the world and with the aura of a legendary innings at Lord's and a war record [he had been a prisoner of war in Germany during the Second World War].

"But Mario brought something else as well. It was the extraordinary spirit of Caversham which had bred sporting success far beyond the reasonable aspirations of a school of that size."

While the wartime matches against Beaumont continued uninterrupted the 1944 fixture was played on Huntley & Palmers' ground at Kensington Road, Reading. This was to avoid the danger from the V2 rockets that were then being sent over London. The Oratory had managed to keep hold of its prestigious cricket fixture in spite of the odds and its doggedness was finally rewarded in 1953 when against

expectations it won comprehensively by 9 wickets. The victory was sealed by James Breaks and Hector Smith who made 173 for the second wicket passing Beaumont's first innings total in the process. It was a fitting climax to the ten years of Father Tomlinson's headmastership and echoed the Oratory's results of the late 1930s.

In 1949 Binyon relinquished his post, prompted by the ironic and typically self-deprecating comment of 'Bones' Headlam: "If you don't leave now, you never will. These things are habit-forming. You'll be stuck here like me for the rest of your life."

Binyon was replaced in his command of the J.T.C. by Lieutenant-Colonel William Hodgson who in 1954 established the Prize that still bears his name.

Barney Webb was replaced as Second Master in 1947 by Frederick Russell 'Pokey' Hoare, who had joined the staff in 1943. He acquired his nickname supposedly from his mannerism of jabbing his finger in argument. The son of an Anglican Bishop of Hong Kong, he had gained a double First in History at Trinity

Right: 'Pokey' Hoare, Second Master, founded the Chess Club (above) and contributed greatly to the intellectual dimension of School life.

College, Cambridge. Hoare brought an intellectual dimension and inspiration to the life of the School which enhanced further Father Tomlinson's efforts to revive it. Soon after his arrival he had taken on the task of running the Library and revived the Debating Society. He also founded and ran a Chess Club. He had played chess for Cambridge and his prowess as a class player at the game was recognised by the boys.

The late 1940s saw the departure from the O.S. scene of two of the figures who had been most active in guiding the School through the difficulties of the decade. In 1947 Lord FitzAlan died at the age of 91. At the time of his death he was the oldest Old Oratorian. In the words of the tribute to him in the *Magazine*:

"It was almost entirely through Lord FitzAlan's determination that the school should retain its independence and its own traditions that, in the face of many difficulties and doubts, the move was made to Woodcote and a new era in our history began."

Above: At CCF camp with Father Tomlinson and Lieutenant-Colonel William Hodgson, 1949.

Then, in 1949, Lord Rankeillour died. He had been a loyal and reliable lieutenant to his uncle, Lord FitzAlan, in his efforts to secure the future of the School.

In 1951, in response to the need for more space and in what turned out to be a further step toward the establishment of a full, traditional house system at the O.S. came the purchase of the building Wayside in the village of Woodcote. It was earmarked as the base for Norris House. The newly appointed Housemaster of Norris House was Patrick Hobson. He had come to the O.S. after a glittering career at St John's College, Cambridge, and was destined to make a crucial contribution to the School over the following decade.

So on the surface all seemed to be going well. As the 10th anniversary of Father Tomlinson's assumption of the headmastership approached he could point to a remarkable achievement. He had with the support of the Governing Body brought the School back from the edge of extinction. Numbers in the School were rising. New facilities were being acquired and developed. A preparatory school had been re-established and was flourishing. The School had come through an official inspection.

However, Tommy's position had been weakened over time in the minds of the Governing Body. His relationships with colleagues were not always the most harmonious. For example, Binyon used to recall how he had often acted as a soothing presence between Tommy and 'Pokey' Hoare when relations between them became fractious. Alexander Baillon, on his resignation as Bursar in 1943, wrote to the Chairman, Lord FitzAlan, complaining of the difficulties of working with his Head Master. This letter remained on the Chairman's file and was produced, together with similar documents, during the unhappy departure of Tommy 10 years later.

Secondly, sound control of financial matters was not Father Tomlinson's strong point. This latter weakness awakened for the Governors a fear of a recurrence of the situation that had brought the School to Woodcote in the first place. The virtual bankruptcy of the end of the Caversham era haunted the thoughts of those in charge of the School's fortunes. So notwithstanding the fact that Father Tomlinson had led the School back from the verge of oblivion, the Governors decided to ask for his resignation, which he tendered in May 1953. News of his impending departure caused dismay among some of the boys as well as among some of the parents. Tommy was naturally sad at having to sever his connection with the School he so loved and whose fortunes he had done so much to restore, but he conducted himself with noteworthy dignity in the period before his departure, not succumbing to any display of bitterness or rancour.

Anthony Cornwell recounted in his booklet *Tommy A Tribute* published to mark his death, how:

"[at] the final morning assembly, before the whole School, the Head Boy B.M.N. Meeson, presented him with their token, a silver tray. When heart speaks to heart, words can become an obstacle. It bore the simplest of inscriptions, To Tommy from the boys of the Oratory School. So moved was he that it took him a little time to regain his composure and express his feelings."

Father Tomlinson cooperated steadfastly with the Governors' wishes during his final term by giving to the person they had designated as his successor the help and assistance they desired from him. Since his successor was Dom Adrian Morey, the Downside monk who was in residence as the School's Chaplain, this could have been a delicate situation. It is to the credit of both that the outcome was successful.

Dom Adrian Morey was eminently fitted for the role of Head Master he now assumed. He had been the Bursar at Downside as well as a Housemaster in the School there. He had also been for a year shortly before the outbreak of the Second World War the Head Master of St Benedict's School, Ealing. Once Dom Adrian had assumed the position of Head Master in September 1953, Downside came doubly to the aid of the O.S. by sending Dom Nicholas Holman as his Bursar. Dom Nicholas possessed a sharp financial and business

Right: The silver salver presented by the boys to Father Tomlinson on his stepping down from the headship in 1953.

acumen which admirably complemented the solid foresight of Dom Adrian.

Dr Henry Will summed up the contribution of Tommy to the O.S. as follows:

"He was, I believe, a headmaster for his times and his remarkable achievement was against the odds to preserve and hand on a tradition and spirit which distinguish the O.S. The survival of the School owed much to him."

In March 1977 a small deputation from the Governing Body pressed Tommy to accept the office of Warden in abeyance since the departure of Father Henry Tristram for the Birmingham Oratory on the closure of Caversham Park in July 1941. He was gratified with the offer but after careful consideration decided instead to accept the offer of becoming the Chaplain of his former pupil John Berkeley at his house, Spetchley Park, near Worcester. So instead of residing at the School as Warden he became its Visiting Confessor. From 1977 until the Michaelmas term of 1984, he would visit the School twice a term staying in St John House for several days. He would say some of the week-day Masses, hear confessions, undertake some sixth form teaching and in the traditional Oratorian manner talk to informal groups of boys in the evenings.

In the final term of his period of such visits he was invited by the Managers of the Monitoring Station to revisit Caversham Park for the first time since he had left it in 1941. So the circle was complete. He was at peace. He died in 1985 in the home for retired priests at Kiln Green, near Reading. He is buried at Spetchley. The hurt of the abrupt manner of his departure from the headship had been assuaged.

CHAPTER NINE

THE ORATORY PREPARATORY SCHOOL

Rose Hill to Great Oaks – the progress of a younger brother

"[E.P.] also wanted … to found a preparatory school where they would be able to prepare boys in the way they wished for the school."

Father Edward Pereira in his Prize Day speech,1924

Right: Rose Hill scenes.

Opposite: Pre-Prep sports day at Great Oaks.

Newman's Oratory School and the Oratory Preparatory School are inextricably linked. In the summer of 1925, three years after the O.S. had moved to Caversham Park, the O.P.S. opened with just four boys at Rose Hill House, a Georgian-style mansion in Emmer Green less than a mile away from the O.S. The first Headmaster was Father Sebastian Ritchie, Head Master of the O.S. from 1921 to 1922. By 1930, there were 39 boys and the School boasted a chapel and sports pavilion. In the early days against the backdrop of a bucolic idyll boys were educated and spiritually nurtured on fresh air, sports, strict discipline and meagre rations.

J.P. McBrien gives his first impression of the establishment that was to become his home:

"No one who had not seen the original setting could imagine the effect on a small boy of that elegant country mansion and the beautifully kept gardens that he was about to become part of …

"We were small but there was a community atmosphere quite unique. Fr Ritchie was strict but fair. One night I participated in a pillow-fight, was caught and had to see the Headmaster the next morning. Yet the night following he came up to our dormitory and treated us to a display of images projected on to the wall by the clever use of his hands against a light …

"We were kept pretty fit. The compulsory run before breakfast was much dreaded, but it helped mould the character! The sports grounds were excellent. When we played host to cricket elevens from other schools we were given strawberries and cream underneath a Cedar of Lebanon."

William F. White gives a boy's view of leaving his
parents and an insight into the youthful preoccupation
with food, or more precisely, lack of it:

*"On the first day of each term we gathered at the Great
Western Hotel at Paddington. We had a quick glimpse
of the massive steam engines, before leaving our parents
or guardians on the platform. We all wore 'Eton' collars,
striped black trousers and black short jackets termed
bum freezers. I remember the very small helpings at
meals. Obesity was no problem, you may be sure …
Mass was compulsory and attended daily. Boxing was
also compulsory and happened several times a week."*

The 1930s O.P.S. was also keen on keeping the boys in
line and luxuries were few and far between. David
Wilson remembers:

*"Discipline was very severe and it is no exaggeration
to say that we were half-starved. Supper regularly
consisted of cold beetroot and a piece of bread. As a
result our world revolved around match teas when
we had the luxury of 'bangers and mash'! Sports
featured very much in school life. Shakespearean
plays in the garden were put on for speech days. SOS
Ritchie, as he was called, was a tall, rather forbidding
Headmaster but in fact completely overruled by the
Matron, who totally dominated the School. "*

Father Ritchie was Headmaster until ill health forced his
retirement in 1938. The Governors, faced with mounting
financial problems, decided to sell Rose Hill and re-
establish the O.P.S. on the top floor of Caversham Park.
So on 20th September 1938 the O.P.S. opened at
Caversham Park with 15 boys and a new Headmaster:
Ronald Richings, formerly Senior English Master at the
O.S. and a respected and popular personality. The
School was entirely separate from the O.S. with the Lady

Chapel reserved for the O.P.S. for the celebration of
Mass and Benediction. By December 1939, Richings
had been elected to the Incorporated Association of
Preparatory Schools and a year later in his Prize Day
address announced that numbers had now reached 52
and would next term be higher.

*Above left: Football team
with D.E.Wilson in front
row, far left and J.B. Stilwell
in the back row, 1937.*

*Below: Outdoor plays
were a highlight of the
summer at Rose Hill.*

Above: Great Oaks today. A scene from Roger Ravenbeard, *the Years 3–4 play.*

Above right: Colts Cricket in the walled garden.

Henry Stilwell welcomed the move to Caversham Park which he noted also brought a change in style of teaching and more importantly diet:

"We fitted into this comparatively small accommodation because we were few in number. This led to a friendly and relaxed atmosphere, fostered by the new Headmaster, in marked contrast to Rosehill which had been rather austere. Another happy contrast was plenty of good food and the luxury of cakes for tea.

"A further source of delight was the superb tuck shop presided over by Sergeant-Major Stanbridge. Stanbridge created further excitement by giving us the opportunity to join in the O.T.C. exercises when, armed with rifles and blank ammunition, we acted as 'enemy' for the O.S. contingent. In 1938 we were all very conscious of the prevailing international tensions. At one stage we were armed with gas masks and would exercise descending to the cellars wearing them. It was not easy stumbling downstairs in the dark wearing a gas mask with a permanently fogged lens!"

In the dark days of 1941 a real crisis came when the Governors decided to sell Caversham Park and accept a house at Downside as a temporary home. The O.P.S. was merged with Worth Preparatory School, also now at Downside. Thus the O.P.S. ceased to exist as an independent entity. Richings resigned to accept an invitation from the War Office to lecture to the troops.

By May 1942 after only two terms at Downside the O.S. had re-established itself in Woodcote. By September 1944 its new Head Master, Father George Arthur Tomlinson (Tommy), had arranged for three cottages in Exlade Street to form a Junior House for a small number of boys aged 10 to 13 prior to their joining the O.S. – a temporary measure until the O.P.S., something very dear to his heart, could be resurrected.

In his Prize Day address of July 1944, Father Tomlinson announced:

"I have always felt that the lack of our own preparatory school has been the cause of the very slow recovery of our numbers since we have been here at Woodcote. That lack will now be partly supplied by the opening of a Junior House for boys of 10 to 13 years of age in the three cottages in Exlade Street. Mr Hoare has taken on the job of launching the new venture, and will act as the first Housemaster, and I am very grateful to him for the valuable work he has already done towards what will, I pray, be an accession of strength to the school."

In 1945 Tomlinson was approached by a Catholic businessman, Bertram Bisgood, owner of The Old Ride formerly an Anglican prep school, at the Branksome end of Bournemouth. Eminently suitable it included a chapel, swimming pool and playing fields at a reasonable asking price. Tomlinson's recommendation to buy was accepted by the Governors.

The new O.P.S. opened in January 1946 with Anthony Patton as Headmaster. Patton was formerly Headmaster of St Anthony's, Eastbourne, whose efforts laid foundations for the O.P.S.'s new existence. In just 12 months numbers increased from 35 to 83 pupils.

In the summer of 1952 with the number of pupils now at 92, Patton resigned to reopen St Anthony's, Hampstead. When he left Tomlinson recalled the difficult days of 1946 and praised Patton as: "a loyal colleague and an outstandingly good Headmaster". He is remembered as the founder of the post-war O.P.S.

His successor Cyril Bull had been Second Master at Ladycross and a fellow pupil of Patton at St Anthony's.

Utterly committed to the welfare of the boys in their care Bull and his wife Auriol opened their home each holiday to boys whose parents were abroad or had died.

Christopher Cook fondly remembers life under the Bull stewardship:

Above left: Service to mark the opening of the O.P.S. at Bournemouth with Father Tomlinson on the far left, 1946.

Above: The Headmaster of O.P.S., Cyril Bull and his wife Auriol.

Left: The Old Ride, Bournemouth.

"Our days were instructive but reassuringly predictable: swimming, table tennis, cricket, darts, trips into the country, cards in the evening, selected TV. We were encouraged to speak our minds on anything and everything, with Cyril gently steering us away from dogmatism, putting his foot down if someone went too far.

"Later I came to realize how much attention they both paid to good manners, lack of pretentiousness, and a positive approach to life. Quite simply we were being educated. With all his insight into the ways of children, Cyril treated us like young adults and we responded."

Like his predecessor Bull left to open his own prep school at Lympne Place in Kent. He was succeeded in 1958 by Christopher Maude who notably raised academic standards and regained Ministry of Education recognition. By July 1967 the number of pupils had risen to 114.

Maude and the O.P.S. in Bournemouth are recalled here by Paul Ketterer, Head Master of All Hallows and a member of staff at the O.P.S. from January 1959, until he joined the O.S. in September 1959:

Right: Entrance to Great Oaks.

Below: Auction house advertisement offering details of the Great Oaks' sale, July 1933.

"My abiding memory of him is first and foremost as a true gentleman of real integrity. He was also exceptionally sensitive to the feelings of his staff and would never ask them to do anything he was not prepared to do himself …

"It really was the most idyllic setting, even when I used to take the 1st XV on training runs before breakfast along the beach and we would break the ice in the puddles as we began the long ascent back up the cliff path to the School."

Maude's retirement at the end of the Christmas term of 1968 coincided with another change of home for the School. Having decided that the two schools should be in much closer proximity with each other, the Governors arranged the sale of Branksome and negotiated the purchase of Great Oaks at Crays Pond, formerly the prep school for St Mary's, Wantage.

So in January 1969 the O.P.S. opened the doors of its new home to 95 pupils, most of whom had moved with the School from Branksome. That Autumn term also saw the arrival of 25 boys from Elston Hall, a prep school near Newark, bringing the numbers of pupils up to 120, the largest there had ever been. It was no easy task for Patrick Stow, the new Headmaster, and his wife Veronica to merge the two schools and in the unfamiliar surroundings of a new home once again create a new O.P.S. It was achieved, however, in a very short space of time.

The boys relished their surroundings: the grounds provided a wonderful adventure playground and the theatre in the Barn was a welcome improvement from Canford Cliffs Village Hall. In 1970 a Pre-Preparatory Department opened with 21 children in two classes and girls admitted for the very first time. The School was rapidly outgrowing the classroom space available so work was begun on a new teaching block, completed in 1973.

Stow resigned in 1977. His successor, George Robertson, had previously been Headmaster of St Martin's School, Yorkshire. Though his tenure was not long, when he and Joan his wife left, he had succeeded in setting up a comprehensive system for pastoral care (the Tutor System) and the School also had a large multi-purpose sports hall.

Robertson was followed in January 1981 by Michael Randell from Claires Court School, Maidenhead. The O.P.S. was in need of a 'shot in the arm' and with the arrival of Michael and Helena Randell that is exactly what it got. All aspects of the School benefited from their energy. The Randells were never happier than when they were engaged on some project: in 1985 new tennis courts were constructed and levelling work commenced on the games field; a link between the sports hall and

classroom block was completed; 1989 saw the conversion of derelict domestic quarters to provide a new music department; the refurbishment of the Barn provided a concert room opened officially in May 1989 by the musicologist Anthony Hopkins; the bronze of Cardinal Newman, commissioned from the sculptress Judy Brown, was unveiled in June 1990; by September that year the Science laboratory, Art and CDT rooms had been completely refitted.

Top left: Early days at Great Oaks.

Top: David Sexon (left) and Michael Randell (second from right) with National Schoolboys' Sevens at Rosslyn Park, 1987.

Above: The old outdoor pool at Great Oaks.

Above: The Barn, opened in 1989 by Anthony Hopkins, who is seated at the piano. On the left is Richard Goodall (Director of Music) and to the right, Michael Randell.

Top right: Violin practice in the Music Department.

Below right: Pre-Prep children hard at work.

Speaking in December 1990 Edward Thorneycroft, Chairman of the Governors, said: "In the last ten years Michael has built up something of which we are extremely proud and we are grateful to him for his single-minded determination to make sure what he and Helena wanted actually took place."

In December 1990 Michael Randell relinquished the reins and in January 1991 David Sexon, Deputy Headmaster since September 1981, became the ninth Headmaster of the O.P.S. In the years which followed Newman's tenet of an all-round education found expression in a high level of academic achievement as well as the blossoming of instrumental and choral music, theatre, the work of the learning support department, the success of the pre-prep, sport for all, trips and tours and the school council. The school became fully co-educational and total numbers grew to over 400 pupils.

was 'perhaps one of the greatest rugby playing prep schools in the country'. First teams in football and hockey also won all their matches that year.

Under Sexon the Pre-Prep was completely rebuilt and the Sports Hall, existing classrooms and Art, Design and Science facilities updated. An Astroturf surface was installed and provision for ICT prioritised. The Thorneycroft Centre (four new classrooms and a school theatre for assemblies and productions), an enlarged library, more classrooms, new and improved staff accommodation, new changing rooms and a new Music School were all completed. Regular trips were established to L'Oratoire, our farmhouse in Normandy.

Sexon often repeated to the children that there were only two school rules: "Do your best and always be kind to each other." Over his 16 years as Headmaster Sexon and his staff were responsible for a generation of fine young men and women educated and nurtured at the O.P.S. A few days before his retirement the schoolchildren and many of his family, friends, colleagues, parents and past pupils came to pay tribute to him.

Above: Girls playing hockey.

Top left: Young artists at work.

Far left: The O.P.S. 1st XV in action.

Spiritual life was enhanced by the appointment in 2001 of Monsignor Antony Conlon as Chaplain. A more flexible approach to boarding for girls as well as boys was introduced. To strengthen the school community through the involvement of parents Sexon also inaugurated the Friends of the Oratory Preparatory School. Frequent fund-raising of all kinds included continued support for our twin school in South Africa.

Memories of Sexon's own *Invicta* rugby teams of 1987 and 1990 and his National Prep School Rugby Sevens Champion side of 1987 were rekindled by the 'Invincibles' of the 2005 1st XV, so that he could say with only a hint of hyperbole that he thought the O.P.S.

Right: Members of the O.P.S. choir sing at the 150th Anniversary Mass in Westminster Cathedral on 2nd May 2009.

Below: The Memorial Window to Thomas, the infant son of Kit and Judy Maude who lost his life in a fire at Branksome in 1965. It was executed by Patrick Reyntiens and was transferred from the Chapel at Branksome to the Chapel at Great Oaks at the time of the School's move. It is based on the window of Our Lady and St Thomas in Bourges Cathedral in France.

When Sexon retired in 2006 he was succeeded as tenth Headmaster of the O.P.S. by Dr Richard Hillier, formerly Housemaster and Head of Classics at Repton School. The school has continued to flourish: the 2008 Ofsted inspection of the Foundation Stage provision concluded: "outstanding in every respect" – a huge tribute in particular to Mrs Chris Gregory, Head of the Pre-Prep Department since 1993. The school was granted International School Award status by the British Council (2008–11) for its inclusion of a global dimension throughout the curriculum; and the number of scholarships and awards gained by leavers in 2007 and 2008 reached an unprecedented total. And new developments continue, with the completion of an adventure playground, indoor swimming-pool complex and pavilion.

In 1990 as the O.P.S. celebrated its 75th anniversary, the Vatican prepared to mark the centenary of the death of its founder, Cardinal Newman, by bestowing on him the title of Venerable. In 2009 as The Oratory School prepares to celebrate its 150th anniversary (and the fortieth of the O.P.S.'s move to Great Oaks) prayers for his beatification and eventual canonisation continue. These prayers were answered on 3rd July, 2009, when the Vatican annnounced its acceptance of the validity of the miracle submitted for the Beatification.

CHAPTER TEN

RESPECTABILITY RETRIEVED

Dom Adrian Morey, 1953–67 and Webster Wilson, 1967–72

"Can I forget? I can never forget."

– Dom Adrian Morey quoting Newman in *Certain Difficulties Felt by Anglicans
in Catholic Teaching* (1850) in his farewell Prize Day speech, 1967

*Opposite: Dom Adrian at
his desk.*

*Below: Dom Adrian at Prize
Giving in 1954 flanked by
Old Boy Marquis du Parc
Locmaria, the Belgian
ambassador, his wife and
Dick Dean on the right.*

When Dom Adrian Morey assumed the
headmastership in September 1953 the School's
finances were once again a cause for concern. A striking
instance of the delicate financial state of the School is
illustrated by the fact that, on assuming the Headship,
Dom Adrian discovered the bank account was empty
and he was forced to sign a cheque on his sister's
account to prevent the gas supply from being cut off.

He wrote to the Chairman outlining further financial
troubles:

*"In the last few days we have been twice telephoned
by the income tax authorities, threatened with
cutting off of the water, and other creditors have
been sending in accounts dating back to 1952 with
strongly worded requests for payment … Yesterday
the Colonel [Hodgson] told me that he would not
prepare for the Term as regards the CCF until he got
his cheque …*

*"I have been very realistic throughout the past
Term [he had been acting as Bursar for that
preceding term] about the school and its needs and I
can't help feeling that if the money cannot be
produced it will be better to close down … I think
that the new Bursar will be as disturbed as I am."*

Dick Dean had given the School a loan to tide it over the
financial hiatus preceding the new Head Master's full
assumption of responsibility for its affairs.

As Dom Adrian pointed out to the Governing Body in
his situation paper at the end of his first year of office:

Far left: The School Library in the Black Room.

Left: Music in the Adam Room with Ronald Tidmarsh.

"I became Head Master a year ago under circumstances that would have discouraged any but the most stout-hearted. The number of boarders in the summer term of last year had been only 77 and the working loss was something like £1,000 a term. There were also tradesmen's bills outstanding amounting to nearly £4,000 …"

Fortunately for the School he did accept the challenge. On his assumption of office the Governors made two important decisions. They decided to put aside firmly any thoughts of looking for another home for the School opting instead for expansion at Woodcote. They also abandoned adherence to the traditional notion that Newman had prescribed a limit to the number of boys there should be in the School. Dom Adrian could now in conjunction with a programme of expansion and improvement of facilities look to increase the numbers with the Governors' blessing.

Although there is no firm evidence for this belief it is certainly true that Newman, when moulding the School in his vision of how it should be run with Ambrose St John and John Norris in the 1860s and 1870s, imprinted on the emerging institution the tradition that it should be of a size that allowed everyone to know everybody else. This point was mentioned by the Inspectors who came to view the School in October 2007. In their report they said that:

"[the] School retains its founder's motto cor ad cor loquitur (heart speaking to heart) and his intention to provide an all-round education which encourages the development of body, mind and spirit. It aims to instil a sense of self-esteem in every pupil and to ensure he is valued as an individual with something to offer at all levels."

Dom Adrian warned the School in September 1953 that changes should be expected. He wisely decided to balance those that he might have expected to be unpalatable, albeit necessary ones in his view, with those designed to raise morale. Dom Adrian was an experienced schoolmaster and a realist.

He introduced a school uniform and removed permission from the Prefects and School Captain to administer corporal punishment. He also, despite the straitened circumstances, purchased a new set of rugby shirts for the 1st XV. Alongside this he arranged for *The Times* to carry a report of the team's match against Douai School. He understood clearly the importance of image and good publicity well before the era of the PR guru. He also knew the value of the proper entertainment of influential people. To this end he needed a suitable venue in the School. He combined the solution of this need with a further role that allowed him to get to know and care for new boys in the School. So he decided that he would base himself at Norris House, the former Wayside, where he could act as the Housemaster of a Junior House. This would serve as a waiting house for boys newly entering the School and so allow him to get to know them and vice versa. Thereby he was subscribing to the Newman

Below: 1st XV 1958. Eric Beagley is on the left and Patrick Hobson is on the right.

spirit of the establishment he now presided over. At Norris House he was able to entertain in a way that he felt was important for the good name and further progress of the School.

Dom Adrian was experienced in rescuing a faltering scholastic institution. This had been his task when he assumed control of St Benedict's School, Ealing, in 1938. So he was aware of the importance of appearances in inviting parents to consider the School as fit for their sons. He was equally aware of the importance of financial stability and attractive facilities in achieving this goal. So together with Dom Nicholas Holman, the Bursar, he set about sprucing up the interior of the place.

In a progress report to the Governors in 1954 he dealt with factors that were predominant at this point:

"A report was spread that Downside had taken the school over (had it done so 90 per cent of my problems would have been removed) and that we were sent the rejects from Worth [then the preparatory school for Downside] and were filling the school with boys of the poorest intellectual quality. This last point is contradicted by the statistics of our intake, which show a remarkable improvement in the intellectual quality of the new boys."

Suspicion that Dom Adrian and Dom Nicholas were Downside plants continued to stalk the efforts of both of them. This suspicion irritated Dom Adrian, as was shown in a letter he wrote to the Chairman: "I am as interested as anybody in killing any idea that the O.S. is a satellite of Downside …"

Dom Adrian's sights were set on attaining election to the Headmasters' Conference. He saw that achievement and the recognition it would imply as an indispensable milestone on the road to recovery. By 1957 he was already taking soundings to this end, conscious that Lord FitzAlan's efforts in 1933 to use his considerable influence and status to gain this *cachet* had met with a rebuff. He was aiming to attain this goal in time for the School's Centenary in 1959.

Good housekeeping on the part of the Head Master and the Bursar had soon brought about the repayment of the overdraft they had inherited. With increasing numbers and under tight financial control the School was soon producing a surplus. By 1954 the total number of boys had broken the 100 mark for the first time since the Caversham era. This made the need for more building increasingly urgent, especially as the existing facilities were patently poor. The science laboratories were described by inspectors for a fund to improve science teaching in independent schools as, "the second worst they had seen in their whole tour". Dom Adrian lamented in retrospect that this fund only gave him: "£1,000 for equipment, while Downside with several modern labs received £13,000." He knew that the "morale of boys suffered when they saw other schools and the Staff needed and deserved better facilities e.g.

warm classrooms". These latter were the three wooden huts erected in the 1940s. They could become so cold that ink would freeze in the inkwells. Boys would sit in them wearing overcoats and gloves, and the electric wiring was unsafe and unreliable.

So, as future prospects began to look encouraging and with the support of the Governors, Dom Adrian began a building programme. Future generations have had cause to be grateful to him for the solid manner in which he built. Despite the pressure on him to have adequate facilities he resolutely refused to compromise on quality of construction. Each of the brick buildings put up during his headmastership was constructed in English bond and with deep foundations. In addition the floors laid down

Above: Entrance to the Walled Garden, the former Kitchen Garden of Woodcote House.

Left: A service in the Chapel.

were made of solid wood blocks to form parquet flooring. Over the years the buildings have required little maintenance, unlike so many constructions of that era.

Change was also coming to the teaching staff. In July 1954 John Norden, who had succeeded Hoare as Second Master in 1950, left to test his vocation in Rome. To replace him Dom Adrian invited Patrick Hobson to return to the O.S. as his Second Master. He had left the staff in July 1953 to teach at Kimbolton School. Hobson was to have a profound influence on the development of the School as Dom Adrian sought to give it viability in the eyes of the outside world. Another sad change in the teaching personnel occurred with the death in June, 1954 of Gerald Headlam.

Fortunately for the School Dom Adrian did not pack up and leave during the difficult early days. His shy and sensitive nature had felt bruised by the lack of understanding he had encountered when he took charge of the School in 1953. Evidence of Dom Adrian's sensitive inner nature is provided by the fact that constantly beside him, wherever he was residing, there was a photograph of Peter McCarthy who had been a boy in the School under him. Peter had on leaving gained a commission in the Royal Marines and was killed in the Suez invasion in November, 1956.

He was not the sort of person who bore a grudge and he had by now been captivated by the Oratory ethos. He continued his work of laying firm foundations for the future of the School.

Below: The old science laboratory.

Bottom: Band practice.

Below right: Centenary Year School Prefects. Igor Judge, School Captain, is on the left, John Hawkes (left) and Jo Vitoria in the centre, Nicholas Kirby on the right.

In 1956 he suffered a setback in his recovery plans when his Bursar, Dom Nicholas Holman, was recalled by Downside. Dom Adrian reacted with customary *sang-froid* at this loss of his key associate and support, remarking that he knew: "he was too good for the O.S. to expect to keep him for long".

By the time the Centenary celebrations of 1959 arrived much had been done towards constructing what is now the heart of the Woodcote campus with the Old House at its core. It was a notable achievement on the part of Dom Adrian and Dom Nicholas to have brought the financial

Above left: Work on the foundations of FitzAlan House, now the Tomlinson Building.

Left: Centenary Year Teaching Staff. To the left of the group is Ronald Tidmarsh (Music), standing holding books is Michael O'Shea (Norris Housemaster), below him in profile is Christopher Lash (FitzAlan Housemaster), seated centre is Patrick Hobson (English, Second Master and Faber Housemaster), behind him are (from the left) Ken Hassall (Chemistry), Angus McCowen (Physics) and Eric Beagley (General Subjects). Behind the Chaplain stand Robert Batley (St John Housemaster) and Stefan Zwierzynski (Mathematics).

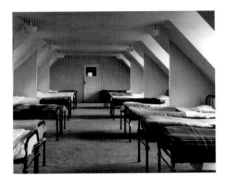

Above (clockwise from top left): The dormitory, the washroom in FitzAlan House, exterior and interior of the new Refectory, now the Library.

situation from its parlous state of September 1953 to the point where in 1956 they were able to embark on building the ground floor of what is now the Tomlinson Building.

It is interesting to note that in his situation paper for the Governors of September 1958, Dom Adrian, in looking ahead, voiced the view that: "[the] House Masters in a lay school should preferably be married men but we have no accommodation of this kind". He was forced for the time being to rely on resident bachelor masters to fulfil that role. He knew that this was not a satisfactory arrangement, but he had no choice. "Given our circumstances this youth and inexperience [of Housemasters] are inevitable and I see no way to avoid it." It was left to his successors to realise his vision of housemasters living on the campus with their families.

Expanding numbers in the School argued the case for the inauguration in 1957 of a new boarding house. It was decided that this additional house be located in the new

wing and be named FitzAlan House in honour of Lord FitzAlan. The new fourth house was put under the charge of a newly-arrived bachelor member of staff, Christopher (Kit) Lash. In concert with Patrick Hobson, Kit Lash supported Dom Adrian's efforts to build up the School by helping to develop its internal life. They left their imprint on the pastoral functioning of the School as well as on its extra-curricular activity in the form of school societies. They also re-laid the foundation for school dramatic activity with their own drama productions leading to the emergence of the Cardinal's Men, the inspired renaming of the O.S. Dramatic Society. This complemented Hobson's efforts to develop the sporting side of school life which by the end of the 1950s were beginning to bear fruit.

Gerard Manley Hopkins' association with the School is commemorated in the name of the Windhover Society (one of Hopkins' sonnets), the Sixth Form society for the reading and discussion of papers. This Society was founded in 1958 by Hobson and Lash. The Windhover Society introduced the tradition of awarding and wearing ties for non-sporting activities to be worn by boys and staff alike. The Society provided the model for the wide array of societies founded at the School in subsequent years. Recognition of Hobson's notable contribution to the School is enshrined in the name of the Society's prestigious annual Patrick Hobson Memorial Lecture. This important event in the School's calendar was started in 1983 after Hobson's death.

With the completion in 1959 of the top storey of FitzAlan House (now the Tomlinson Building), other building projects came rapidly on stream. Norris House moved into this storey while Faber (top floor) and St John (first floor) occupied the Old House. A new refectory (now the Library) was completed in 1958 followed by a new swimming pool a year later. A squash court and two new tennis courts were installed. The improving financial situation of the School had allowed for these developments. There had also been an appeal for funds

ahead of the Centenary celebrations, headed by the Duke of Norfolk, which provided extra building capital.

So, as the 100th anniversary of the foundation approached, the horizon began to brighten and in 1959 numbers in the School exceeded 200 for the first time ever. The Centenary itself was marked by a solemn High Mass at Brompton Oratory on 21st April, the celebrant being Father Stephen Dessain, the Provost of the Birmingham Oratory. The Archbishop of Birmingham, the Most Reverend Francis Grimshaw, delivered the homily.

The Archbishop also paid the School a visit during this special year. On 5th July he administered the Sacrament of Confirmation and on the previous day he stood in for the Duke of Norfolk as Prize Giver. The Duke had, as Dom Adrian phrased it in his speech: "been struck down with the suitably ducal complaint of gout". Earlier the Archbishop had informally opened the new swimming pool.

There was an Old Boys cricket match on the following day and the weekend's events were rounded off on the Monday with an Inspection of the CCF by General Sir Francis Festing.

The new swimming pool was joined in 1960 by a gymnasium-cum-theatre which had its first public dramatic performance, Shakespeare's *Julius Caesar*, on the evening of Prize Day 1961. Gradually Dom Adrian was assembling an impressive range of buildings for the School. A new Chapel was also planned alongside these developments and money was indeed collected for its building. Mrs Niggli, the mother of Willy, presented to the School silver candlesticks to furnish it. She was overheard one day expressing her impatience at the lack of action about the Chapel, saying: "I wish Father Adrian would hurry up and build the Chapel. I have reserved the marble for the altar and the mountain is running out."

Above: CCF, 1959.

Mrs Niggli was a byword for her lavish generosity to people connected with the School. She would, for example, bring liqueur chocolates for Father Adrian's dog. He would hand them on quietly to his Secretary, the reliable and efficient Mrs Bobbie Everitt, saying: "These are too good for Honey. You take them."

Under an initiative of the Old Boys a new cricket pavilion was being provided for the main cricket field. This was formally opened in June, 1963, when to mark the occasion Patrick Hobson, the former Second Master, led a strong Invitation XI against the School XI.

In 1962 Dom Adrian achieved his goal of obtaining election to the Headmasters' Conference. It represented a crowning endorsement of his efforts over the previous nine years. As the *Magazine* of 1961–62 put it: "[no] Headmaster is elected unless his school is recognised by the committee as having reached a high level of academic attainment and also as having acquired a very definite status in the public eye."

Sport was a priority. After distributing the prizes in 1962, Duke Bernard began his speech with words that echoed the O.S. of earlier days, saying: "I am not

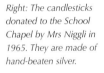

Right: The candlesticks donated to the School Chapel by Mrs Niggli in 1965. They are made of hand-beaten silver.

interested in whatever academic arrangements you may have here. I am interested in the cricket. It matters to me whether The Oratory wins or loses at Lord's."

The Duke's love of cricket and his renowned organisational skills, as demonstrated in the planning and execution of the Coronation of Her Majesty Queen Elizabeth II in 1953, led to the invitation to him to be Manager of the M.C.C. tour of Australia in 1962. The B.B.C. satirical programme, *That Was The Week That Was*, seized on this fact for a musical parody, based on the song of Sir Joseph Porter (Now I'm ruler of the Queen's Navy), in the Gilbert and Sullivan operetta, *H.M.S. Pinafore*. The first lines of the parody ran: "When I was young I played the fool, batting in the nets at the Oratory School", the refrain went: "And now I'm Manager of the M.C.C. "

The School's cricket, thanks to the patient efforts of Patrick Hobson, was now enjoying a purple patch which must have delighted His Grace and which echoed the outstanding achievements of D.C.F. Burton in the late 1930s. Hobson's persistent emphasis during the 1950s on developing in the School's cricket and rugby what he called "a winning ethic", was now coming to satisfying fruition.

In 1961 the 1st XV had enjoyed "the most successful season for many a long year". The 1st XI had already clinched an exciting victory at Lord's in 1960 by 26 runs to be followed a year later by a more emphatic one by 93 runs. The result in 1962 was a deserved culmination of Hobson's stewardship of the game at the O.S. The XI won by an innings and 21 runs. As the *Magazine* of 1961–62 commented, it was: "a fitting climax for Mr Hobson who left the School at the end of this term and to whom the team owes much for his constant and patient advice and assistance". He had laid the foundations for post-war O.S. sport well and they would be built upon

and developed effectively in ensuing years leading up to the granting of *The Daily Telegraph's* Independent School for Sport Award in 2007.

The Lord's match in 1963 won by the O.S. by 116 runs was notable for the century scored by Tommy Peirce, the Oratory captain. The Lord's matches in the two subsequent years were both drawn and then in 1966 Beaumont defeated The Oratory by 8 wickets. This was a fitting note for this fixture to end on. In that year the Jesuits had taken the decision to close Beaumont College. They planned to focus their educational resources in the independent sector on Stonyhurst College in Lancashire. After much discussion with the Lord's authorities Downside School took over the place of Beaumont in the sole Lord's fixture between Catholic public schools. This led to the exciting match of 1967. After The Oratory had scored 164 runs, Downside at 128 for 3 wickets seemed to be heading for a first Lord's victory. Then, as the *Magazine* reported:

Right: Sergeant-Major Alfred Gillham headed up the CCF for 25 years. He was instrumental in building up shooting as a sport and the new shooting range (below), opened in 1999, was named in his honour.

"… the drama began. The vital overs were bowled [in which three key wickets fell] … The crowd was now abuzz with excitement and anticipation. Three balls later [another wicket fell] and Downside were reeling; having slumped from 128 for 3 to 144 for 7. The damage was done, the last three Downside men offered but token resistance … and the Oratory had won an amazing and tremendously exciting victory."

The 1968 match was drawn and was destined to be the final one in the fixture. The reorganisation of cricket by the sport's authorities led to the discontinuation of the schools fixtures at Lord's. So an occasion which had been of major assistance in The Oratory's post-war attempt to recover its fortunes succumbed to the march of progress.

Over the coming years the CCF was to prove a headache for Dom Adrian. He did wonder whether it was too expensive to retain and hence ought to be disbanded. In the end he was persuaded to appoint a Sergeant Major Instructor. This was Alfred Gillham of the Welsh Guards who arrived on the staff in May 1967 and, with a short break, continued as a much loved and respected member of staff until his retirement in 1992. He put the CCF on an even keel and laid the basis of its present flourishing state. He also built up the sport of shooting. In recognition of his contribution to the School, the new shooting range, opened in May 1999, was named the Alf Gillham Range in his honour.

Dom Adrian's achievement in getting the outside world to respect the O.S. was gathering pace at the beginning of the 1960s. New buildings were appearing,

the School was running at a surplus, a lively teaching staff was being built up, the number of boys was still rising. In 1962 the roll had reached 235 in number and the previous year's surplus had been £20,200. Over the 14 years of his headship some £280,000 had been spent on buildings and development.

During the 1960s The Oratory began to expand its portfolio of sports. In 1962 rowing was introduced, the School arranging to borrow boats from Reading Rowing Club. Then in 1968 Association Football was restored to the School for the first time since it had been discontinued upon the move to Caversham Park in 1922.

Having achieved notable successes Dom Adrian decided to retire at the end of the 1966–67 academic year. In his retirement he spent two years at Little Malvern in Worcestershire as the Parish Priest before moving to Benet House in Cambridge. From there he conducted an effective Benedictine presence in the University. He died in 1989. Dom Adrian is remembered for steering the financial rescue in 1953, for getting the outside world to take the School seriously again and for overseeing the construction of many of the school buildings. He left it in 1967 in a healthy state on which future generations could build and have indeed built.

After much deliberation the Governors decided to appoint Mr Webster Wilson, the Second Master, to replace Dom Adrian as Head Master. He took on a school whose finances were in a robust state. Wilson's perceptive appreciation of the situation of the School he was now in charge of, is shown in a memorandum he wrote for the Governors in 1970 which anticipates many of the developments of later years:

"The appeal of the Oratory should increase, provided that it is developed along the right lines. By this I mean that the special characteristics of the school should be developed to their logical conclusion, e.g., by aiming at a proper system of houses with resident housemasters, etc., and by exploiting the feminine influence to which Newman rightly attached great importance. For economic reasons this cannot be done all at once, but there is no reason why, with proper planning, it should not be done gradually or that it should be more costly than any other mode of development."

Above: This portrait of Dom Adrian Morey by Julia Hesletine is considered by many to capture the essence of his personality.

This outline for the development of the School was prophetic in tone and anticipated much that was to follow in the next 30 years. Unfortunately the money was not available for him to put his vision into effect.

An important step in the re-establishment of the financial infrastructure of the Association was the setting up in 1971 of the Oratory Schools Foundation. This was the brainchild of James Comyn, at this time a member of the Governing Body. Its aim was to build up a fund whose capital would provide help with fees in necessitous circumstances.

Right: Webster Wilson (wearing spectacles) with a group of Upper School boys smoking pipes. Allowing boys to smoke pipes created much press coverage and Wilson defended the School's decision robustly: 'But all the evidence leads us to believe that cigarettes are the main problem and that pipe-smoking is relatively harmless. I should like to add here, that our School Medical Officer is entirely in favour of the rule.'

Tom McIntyre worked under Webster Wilson and knew him well. In 2008, he viewed his headmastership:

"It was not an easy time. Wilson, an Irish convert of presence and authority with a successful headship behind him, had seen on appointment that the school, much expanded under Dom Adrian Morey, urgently needed a corresponding re-evaluation of aims, structures and standards. Although many of the Common Room and parents agreed, Wilson's uncompromising methods, unbending contempt for bad custom, … had alienated some Old Oratorians, suspicious of change, and some Governors, who feared for the school's gentlemanlike atmosphere and newfound financial stability. Worse, it antagonised less perceptive Oratorians."

So the Governors became unhappy with Wilson's control of matters in the School. The number of boys in the School was declining and the School's reputation among preparatory schools was on the wane. There were distinct echoes of 1953 in the situation but with the added difference of a greater accountability as the School was now a member of the Headmasters' Conference. The

Chairman offered the dormant post of Warden to Dom Adrian to keep an eye on matters. Dom Adrian was now firmly settled as Head of Benet House at Cambridge so he declined the offer, though he did accept a seat on the Governing Body. Eventually, worried by falling numbers and no doubt haunted by the memory of earlier crises, the Governors sought Webster Wilson's resignation in 1972. He moved on to become Head Master of the Bishop Walsh Secondary School in Sutton Coldfield and gradually lost contact with The Oratory.

The Governors were now faced with the problem of who his successor should be. They turned to an internal candidate and their choice fell on Adrian Snow, Housemaster of FitzAlan House since 1967. Snow had been appointed to the staff by Dom Adrian Morey in 1966 and had impressed him at the time as a potential candidate for preferment. He was offered the post initially on a temporary basis but was confirmed in it in 1973, after two terms as Acting Head. On this occasion the genius of The Oratory for alighting on the right person at the right moment had come into play. Adrian Snow saw the justice of some of Webster Wilson's ideas and insights about the School and his experience of the School under Dom Adrian allowed him to marry these with the latter's development skills. In his headmastership he moved Dom Adrian's work forward and also brought his own, deep rooted vision. As noted by a member of staff, Ian McLean:

"… he was not the kind of Headmaster who would let the School stand still, and he was not the type of Headmaster who would fall for the other temptation of being frivolously with it. Adrian's vision was quite different in that the development of the School should proceed in a way that was in harmony with Newman's ideas. The spiritual and academic needs of the individual had to be addressed in a structure that was relevant and civilizing."

CHAPTER ELEVEN

RECOVERY CONTINUES

Adrian Snow, Maurice Lynn and Simon Barrow, 1972–2000

"Every pupil must be encouraged to achieve something outside the necessary academic passes."
– Adrian Snow's mantra to his Housemasters

Opposite: Rowing was introduced to the School in 1962. It now has its own boathouses on the Thames between Whitchurch and Mapledurham. The Boat Club competes each year at Henley Regatta.

Right: School photo with Adrian Snow in the centre. Next to him on the left are firstly Pat O'Malley and then Stefan Zwierzynski, who both served as Second Master. To the right of him are firstly Bill Oliver, a long-standing member of staff, and Tom McIntyre, Head of Classics and Housemaster of St John House.

Adrian Snow had joined the teaching staff in September 1966 from Brighton College. He had been educated at Hurstpierpoint College where he had been a promising athlete and games player. Like his predecessor he had been a student at Trinity College, Dublin. In September 1967 he took over as the Housemaster of FitzAlan House. He was also the Head of the History Department as well as being Master in charge of Cricket. So he came to the O.S. headship with the perspective of other schools behind him and with a solid working knowledge of the ways of The Oratory, as well as an awareness of its current situation and needs.

On assuming the reins of office Snow sought to raise the academic ambitions of the School. He was also convinced that more building development on the campus was needed to catch up with rival schools. To achieve the first ambition he aimed to reinforce the teaching staff. A new pay scale and improved conditions of service were introduced. Steps were taken to ensure that good practitioners were retained. It became the norm for members of the Common Room to think of staying for the whole or greater part of their careers. This had an effect on academic standards. The era was ending when, as during the Caversham period and under Tommy's headship, the School could afford to look askance at academic results and achievement, although both eras could point to examples of high academic success. A revision of the system of options was brought in and the form structure within the School was updated including the removal of some surviving anachronisms. For example it ceased to be a privilege to belong to the Sixth Form.

Left: Biology lesson.

Alongside his development of the internal workings of the School, Snow did not lose sight of his long-term ambition to improve accommodation for the boys and the staff. The former entailed a complex exercise in relocating the boarding houses as new premises were arranged. Paradoxically this problem was made easier by the 1973 introduction of a Junior Department of two forms with an 11-year-old entry. This initiative was housed in the Newman wing at its beginning and then in the former Junior House, Wayside, in the South Stoke Road in Woodcote. The present purpose-built accommodation on the Back Drive, since renamed St Philip's House, was ready for it in 1974. It was later divided into two sections, Pereira House and Dean House, honouring these two important figures in the School's history.

More and better living space for boys and House staff soon began to appear. It was of paramount importance at this stage to have a new Refectory and Chapel, into which all the steadily increasing number of boys including the new 11-year-old entry could fit at one time. These were ready in 1977. It was a major achievement to accomplish this re-invigoration of the

New buildings during Adrian Snow's headship; boarding houses, Refectory and the Chapel.

campus at a time of considerable national financial uncertainty. That was partly the result of an appeal for funds and also of the imaginative use of the skills of the Clerk of the Works, Jan Kisiel and his team, but mostly the product of effective financial control and keeping a good balance between income and expenditure.

Much re-siting of amenities took place at this time. The upshot of this breathless exercise was that the School's necessary "catching up phase" was completed. It is a tribute to the robustness of the O.S. under Snow that it could transcend the upheavals involved and flourish.

Parallel with this external development went internal evolution. Music enjoyed a renaissance based on a

Left: Student in the new Art Studio in the 1970s.

Far left: Current art students.

Below left: The Cadet Force expanded under Adrian Snow's leadership, with an RAF Section and here, in a capsize drill in the swimming pool, a Royal Navy Section.

newly built Music School. Art followed suit also in new premises. Long gone were the days when these subjects depended on part-time directors. The CCF also began to burgeon. New Sections were formed. Growing numbers in the School made this expansion feasible and Major Gillham's efficient direction had made the Force an attractive option for boys because of its emphasis on challenging adventure activities. The proud service tradition of the School was being maintained.

In 1973 Stefan (Zulu) Zwierzynski retired as Second Master. He continued his service to the School as the Housemaster of Junior House and Head of the Mathematics Department. He was succeeded as Second Master by Pat (Pom) O'Malley who resided in the newly kitted-out staff flat in the Old House, once occupied by the whole of St John House. Snow's vision of resident, married housemasters was on the way to being realised. These two members of staff helped Snow to set the benchmarks in the areas of school life he was anxious to upgrade; Zulu in the classroom with his determined commitment in the setting of professional standards; Pat in the pastoral life of the School as a caring housemaster of Faber House, ably supported by his wife, Moira.

Right: Junior House boys with Pat Connolly and (far right) making models.

Above: The bust of Duke Bernard in the Front Hall.

Right: Edward Thorneycroft (O.S. 1941–4), Chairman of Governors from 1977–98.

March 1973 saw the institution of another regular feature of the O.S. annual cycle, namely the Catholic Preparatory Schools Rugby Sevens Tournament, an event organised by Simon Barrow. Through this event the O.S. was able to show to the Catholic preparatory school world that it was recovering its composure and was on the way to becoming a force to be reckoned with.

In January 1975 Duke Bernard died. With his passing The Oratory lost not just one of its leading alumni but also someone who had stuck by it through thick and thin. Like his uncle, Viscount FitzAlan, he had used his considerable clout readily in favour of the School; fronting appeals to support its development, putting words into the right ears on its behalf, happily presiding at events. He had served his old School well in its moment of need. He was followed, in 1977, as President of the Association by Dick Dean, who was replaced as Chairman of the Governing Body by Edward Thorneycroft.

Dean's name is remembered at the School for the school prizes he instituted in 1965. That year at the suggestion of Dom Adrian Morey he gave money for two prizes to be awarded for laudable industry and effort by students in arts and science subjects. They continue to this day. A more lasting memorial to him is the financial stability of the School, indeed its very survival against the odds. If anyone had ever had any qualms about Dean's judgment in such matters in the early days, when all seemed without hope, they would have done well to recall a comment about him by his

Secretary: "Don't worry about Mister Dick. Everything he touches turns to gold."

Aside from The Oratory School and allied to it, another of Dean's enthusiasms that took up much of his attention later in his life was the cause for the beatification and eventual canonisation of the School's Founder. In 1975 he

was influential in the formation of a society to further those ends. This society was *The Friends of Cardinal Newman* based at the Birmingham Oratory. In 1981 he was also instrumental in establishing the American equivalent based at the University of Notre Dame, Indiana. When Dean died in 1982, he was succeeded as President by Sir James Comyn, by then a High Court Judge.

Comyn had resigned from the Governing Body in 1983 and remained as President of the Association until poor health forced him to give up the post in 1990. His successor was Miles, 17th Duke of Norfolk, who had inherited the title from his second cousin, Bernard. Although educated at Ampleforth both his father and grandfather were Old Oratorians and he showed himself

more than willing to continue his family's close involvement with the School.

The O.P.S. also had changes of Head Master around the same time as Adrian Snow's appointment in 1972. In 1977 Patrick Stow stepped down in favour of George Robertson, the successful Head Master of St Martin's School, Yorkshire. Sadly ill health forced Robertson to relinquish this post at the beginning of 1981 when he was succeeded by Michael Randell. In 1986 he joined the staff of The Oratory School. He was a talented ball player and also an enthusiastic golfer having been Secretary of a golf club in Germany in the interim between his services at the two schools. He sowed the germ of the idea of a school golf course in the mind of Snow when the latter was seeking ways of expanding and upgrading the School's sports portfolio. Ill health forced a final retirement from teaching on Robertson in early 1991.

This improvement of the School's sporting facilities had followed the acquisition of more land for playing fields alongside the Woodcote by-pass built in 1972.

Above: The Golf Course, which was initiated by George Robertson in 1987.

Left: Sir James Comyn (O.S. 1933–8). He set up the Oratory Schools Foundation in 1971 and was President of the Association from 1983 to 1990.

Right: The menu cover for the retirement luncheon of Adrian Snow in April 1989.

The School could host a full set of visiting fixtures with other schools at all ball games. In the previous year the swimming pool had been covered and heated. In 1984 two new boathouses, one wet for coaching launches and one dry for storing the boats, were completed.

A clue to the rising quality of the teaching and pastoral staff is given by the fact that several members of staff appointed by Snow and made Housemasters by him moved on to headmasterships. Indeed it was jocularly commented by one member of staff that the reason Ratcliffe College had failed to find a satisfactory candidate for its headship at this time was that there was no Oratory housemaster in the application list. The School's confidence in itself was rising.

Academic results were also improving culminating in the winning of a number of Oxford open entrance awards in 1983. In 1984–5 a new block was built by the Works Department alongside the present Tomlinson Building to house the newly introduced teaching of Computing and Information Technology. This building was an example of the creative deployment of that department to improve facilities with the least strain on the school finances. Another such project completed by the in-house works staff was the building of the pavilion for the newly levelled Lower Field.

The emptying of Wayside through the rehousing of the boarding houses at the main school gave the opportunity to capitalize on the real estate value of that building and its plot. Its extensive garden had been sold in the early 1970s. The original house was sold and the adjoining wing turned into residential accommodation for members of

staff. The Chapel had been replaced by another building further along the South Stoke Road. More staff accommodation became available and the School built up an impressive range of living units on its campus also wisely acquiring a buffer zone between itself and the new housing developments appearing on the edge of Woodcote.

A much respected member of the teaching staff of this era was Zygmunt Chojecki who died in 1983. He was a Visiting Teacher of Russian and Italian at the O.S. in addition to lecturing at R.M.A. Sandhurst and serving as a Monitor at the B.B.C. Monitoring Station at Caversham Park. It was remarkable that someone who only taught part-time should achieve the level of respect within the School that he did.

The success of Adrian Snow in all his improvement work persuaded the Governors to award him sabbatical leave during the academic year of 1981–82 to recharge his batteries and to refresh his perspective on the School.

During Snow's absence his duties were covered by Simon Barrow who had been appointed Deputy Head Master in succession to Pat O'Malley in 1980 on the latter's retirement and move to the headship of the Junior Department. This latter position was filled on Pat's final retirement in 1982 by Tom McIntyre, who served the O.S. devotedly until his own retirement in 1986.

In 1988, Adrian Snow decided that it was time for him to give up the reins of office. However the Governors were reluctant for the School to lose his vision of development and his ability to make it a reality, so they invited him to

Luncheon
in honour of
the Retirement of
Adrian Snow
Headmaster of the Oratory School
1973 - 1988

Claridges

Monday, 24th April 1989

continue in the service of the School as Warden, reviving the post for the first time since Father Henry Tristram's return to the Birmingham Oratory in 1941.

As ever at the O.S. the appointment of a new Head Master posed a challenge for the Governors. Experience had shown that apart from being a practising Catholic and familiar with boarding school education, the person appointed would need to be open to the O.S. spirit. Their choice fell on Maurice Lynn. Lynn had formerly been a member of the O.S. teaching staff which he had joined in 1973 from Magdalen College, Oxford. He had taken easily to the O.S. way of doing things and there was keen regret amongst boys and colleagues alike when in 1979 he decided to move on to a more senior post at Radley College. That had led to the Headship of the French Department at Westminster School, from where he applied to be Adrian Snow's successor.

Lynn brought a gentler, more reticent style to the headmastership. However, behind him Snow continued in his position as Warden with the development work that he had initiated as Head Master.

The highlight of Lynn's headmastership took place in 1990. That year saw the School's contribution to the national events to mark the centenary of the death of Cardinal Newman. The aim of the School's activity was to remind the world of Newman scholarship of the then largely overlooked fact that he had founded a school in addition to the University in Dublin and the Birmingham Oratory. The intention was to focus the School's own event on one single day as close as possible to the anniversary of its foundation. The day chosen was 2nd May, 1990. The day began with a Solemn Mass at which the Apostolic Pro-Nuncio, His Excellency Archbishop Luigi Barbarito, was present and robed on the Sanctuary. After lunch guests and members of the School could view the 'Newman in his School' exhibition mounted in the Black Room.

A special booklet, *Newman's Idea of a School* by Dr Andrew Nash (Head of English 1984–2001), was

published by the School on this day. Newman's ideas on university education were already well-known through his work *The Idea of a University*, based on his writings produced when he was trying to set up the Catholic University of Ireland in Dublin in the 1850s. However he left no such document to express his vision about education of the young.

Many who know the School well regard it as the organic, constantly evolving substitute for that treatise on secondary education by one of the world's most respected thinkers on education, informed by the Christian values of the founder of the Congregation of the Oratory, St Philip Neri. Newman never planned to

Above: Edward Thorneycroft, Chairman of Governors, Rt Rev. Monsignor Vaughan Morgan CBE, Chaplain to the School 1984–97 (O.S. 1947–9) and Maurice Lynn, Head Master.

Scenes from the celebrations to mark the centenary of Cardinal Newman's death, May 1990:

Right: Henry Will and David Wilson chatting to guests.

Far right: Mrs Edie Fitzherbert-Brockholes with Father David Sillince.

Right: Scenes from the Solemn Mass, 2 May 1990.

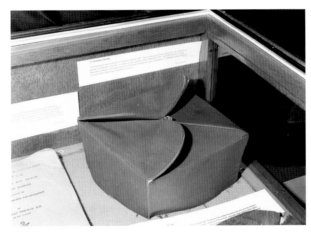

Right: Part of the Centenary Exhibtion featuring items from the School's Archive such as Newman's biretta and early records.

write such a work. However, glimpses of his intentions in this area can be gleaned from accounts of the School in his lifetime, from his letters and writings about it, from reminiscences of boys who were in it under him. Dr Nash's work was an attempt to put down on paper Newman's vision of what the School should entail as he moulded the institution with the assistance of Ambrose St John and John Norris, in the wake of the Darnell Affair.

In 1990 it was time for the outside world to be told how that vision had survived through all the crises and vicissitudes of its history.

The events of 2nd May, 1990 concluded with a performance by the orchestra and chorus of the Cambridge University Musical Society of *The Dream of Gerontius*, Elgar's setting of the poem written by Newman in 1865 at a time when he was most preoccupied with resettling the School after its uncertain beginning. The CUMS chorus and orchestra performed under the baton of Stephen Cleobury. They were struck by the response of an audience for whom the words of the poem were of greater significance than for many of their previous audiences. This performance fitted appropriately into the School's Newman Centenary Music Festival which ran from the end of April 1990 until the Open Day Concert on 26th May.

The culminating event of the national Newman year was an ecumenical service held in St Paul's Cathedral, London on 23rd November, 1990. The address was given by the Reverend Doctor John Newton, Free Church President of Churches Together in England. In welcoming all those present the Dean of St Paul's read a message from Pope John Paul II. The occasion could have given no clearer demonstration of the universal respect and veneration in which Cardinal Newman is held throughout the whole Christian world.

Lynn presided over these events with calm and sensitivity. During his headmastership The Oratory embarked on another departure which fitted in with his Francophile interests. It purchased a base in Normandy

nowadays referred to as L'Oratoire. This was a converted farmhouse near the town of Aunay-sur-Odon, south of Bayeux. It has provided a base for study visits for groups from both the O.P.S. and the O.S.

The house in France formed just one part of the School's development at this time. Under the guidance and supervision of Adrian Snow a new Sports Centre was constructed around the recently covered swimming pool, comprising squash courts and two sports halls. The smaller of

Above and top: Real Tennis. The smaller of the two sports halls in the Sports Centre became a Real Tennis court, in which the 2006 World Championship took place.

Left: Five-a-side football in the large Sports Hall.

these halls became a Real Tennis court, an innovative venture for a school at this period. The commissioning of the new, larger, sports hall allowed the old gymnasium to be refurbished as the School Theatre. It also gave a large space in which public examinations could be efficiently conducted.

In 1991 the School's Newman Year closed with news from Rome that the Founder was to be declared a 'Venerable Servant of God'. So the climax of the year's activity to mark the centenary of the death of the Founder was fitting: he had reached the first stage on the route to canonisation.

In the course of 1991 Lynn came to the conclusion that his "natural habitat was the classroom and not the office", and he had the moral courage to state this publicly and resign his position. The *Magazine* wrote of his headmastership: "During his three years as Headmaster, Maurice Lynn will be remembered for his scholarly gentleness, kindness and for his unstinting efforts to raise the profile and reputation of the Oratory."

Right: Simon Barrow spent the large part of his teaching career at The Oratory School, serving as Housemaster, Deputy Headmaster and, from 1992 to 2000, as Head Master. He died in 2006.

As the Governors had recently exhaustively combed the field for a successor to Adrian Snow, they decided to turn to the Deputy Head Master, Simon Barrow, to fill the post. Barrow was reluctant but finally agreed after much persuasion from some of the Governors. He took over in January 1992. Probably the most pertinent comment on his appointment was made by the *Magazine*, quoting *The Daily Telegraph's Schools Guide*: "which spoke of his loyalty and of his being steeped in the ethos of the School."

Barrow had joined the teaching staff in 1969 as an historian. He acted as House Tutor in St John House and in 1971 became the Housemaster of Norris House. He was to become the longest serving Housemaster at Woodcote. He produced successful school plays, such as *The Royal Hunt of the Sun*; he frequently refereed rugby matches and he had organised the Oratory School Catholic Preparatory Schools Sevens Tournament each Lent term since its inception. He knew the School through and through and it was only his sense of loyalty towards it that allowed him to overcome his reluctance to step up from being its Deputy Head Master, as he had been since 1980, to become its chief officer.

Simon Barrow had been educated at Stonyhurst College. The flexible, easy-going style of The Oratory suited him and he took to it as soon as he arrived on the staff in 1969 from Caldicott Preparatory School, after reading History at the University of Reading.

Simon Barrow's great contribution to The Oratory School was with the support of the Governing Body, to steer it through the uncertain times of the national recession of the early 1990s. He also steered it through the first effects of national educational bureaucracy. National inspections of the School were no strange phenomenon; indeed there had been one before the First World War in 1910.

Barrow took pains to improve the facilities he had inherited as well as to underline the School's history and pedigree. A memorial was erected on the edge of the

In November of each year a party from the O.S. and O.P.S. calls at Caversham Park on their way to the Annual Requiem Mass for deceased Old Oratorians at the Little Oratory, London. They lay a wreath at the memorial and a brief service is held.

In 1996 a new three-manual Allen organ was installed in the Chapel. This was made possible largely as a result of a most generous donation by Father John Tolkien to commemorate a century of his family's connection with the Fathers of the Birmingham Oratory and with the School. In the meantime the embellishment of the former Old Chapel, now St Joseph's, proceeded and the project, together with the new entrance porch, was ready in the Summer of 1994. Its former altarpiece was also restored. This is a copy of the altarpiece of the Chapel of the Medici-Riccardi Palace in Florence which depicts the Madonna and Child in a symbolic wooded landscape. The Oratory altarpiece was presented to the School in memory of Brigadier-General George Pereira who died at Kanze,

Above: The Pereira altarpiece in the Chapel. It was presented to the School in memory of Brigadier-General George Pereira (O.S. 1876–83), the elder brother of E.P.

Far left: A new organ was donated to the Chapel by Father John Tolkien (O.S. 1931–6) in 1996.

cricket field to remind people that the field itself was the School's memorial to all those connected with the School who had served in the Second World War and a tribute to those who had lost their lives in that conflict.

Another memorial erected in 1999 to mark an important aspect of the School's past was the memorial next to the graves that still lie near to the former School Chapel at Caversham Park. Its inscription reads: "Caversham Park was the home of The Oratory School from 1922 to 1941. The building opposite was the School Chapel, built as a tribute to all Old Oratorians who served in the First World War and as a memorial to the 87 among them who gave their lives. Behind this plaque are the graves of three Oratorians who died while still boys in the School."

Above: Edward Thorneycroft and David Wilson unveiling the re-sited gateposts, 1999.

Above right: The gateposts were cut off from the School in the 1970s by the construction of the Woodcote by-pass.

Szechuan Province, China on 20th October, 1923. At the time of his death the War Memorial Chapel at Caversham was being built. In his memory his family presented two tapestries and this Altarpiece to the new Chapel. At Caversham this latter was hung above the altar, sometimes known as the Lady Altar, later used for worship by the O.P.S. Unlike the tapestries it survived the chapel fire at Woodcote on 18th October, 1942 where it was the main altarpiece. It now occupies that position in the main Chapel. It is signed H.J. Bueno de Mesquita, Firenze 1924 after Neri di Bicci.

The gateposts at the former entrance to the Front Drive had been isolated when the Woodcote by-pass had been routed past the front of the School. They were now re-erected at the top of the Front Drive to replace the pillars which formerly stood there and which had been constantly damaged by vehicles negotiating the narrow space between them. The gateposts were re-sited there as a memorial to the thirty boys who came to Woodcote House in May 1942 under the headmastership of Gerald (Bones) Headlam to restart the O.S. after its two-term sojourn at Downside. They were unveiled by Edward Thorneycroft (Chairman of the Governing Body) on 28th April, 1999. This was his last appearance at a School function before his death on 16th April, 2000. He was devoted to the School and had served it selflessly since becoming Secretary of the Oratory School Society in 1949. His son Lieutenant-Colonel Tom Thorneycroft

(Governor 1998–2007) performed another opening ceremony at the School that year for the Alf Gillham Shooting Range which had been erected alongside new CCF buildings.

Extensions to St John House and FitzAlan House were constructed, the Theatre was revamped, improvement work was carried out for the Art Department, the Pavilion received more changing room space, a refurbishment of the Science Laboratories was begun entailing an addition to the south face of the Morey Building.

An extension to the dry boathouse was built and opened by Duke Miles of Norfolk, President of the Association, on 31st May, 1997. He startled those present to witness his cutting of the ribbon by commenting, as he looked around at the names of the racing boats on the racks: "Never thought I'd see *Cardinal Newman* bunked on top of the *Duchess of Norfolk*. Same bloody shelf too."

In his Prize Day speech of 1999 Simon Barrow announced his intention to retire at the end of the following academic year. The newly-refreshed Governing Body took the decision when considering his replacement, to break new ground and to look for his successor outside the Oratory community. They set their face against an appointment from within, as had up till then through force of circumstances been the case. They were rewarded for their outwardness by receiving a total of 21 applications from good class candidates. They were advised in their deliberations by Jonty Driver, Master of Wellington College. He had been so intrigued by the post that he found time in a busy schedule to take part in the interviewing process. The successful candidate was Clive Dytor, a Housemaster at St Edward's School, Oxford, and former Royal Marine who had served with distinction in the Falklands War.

READY FOR THE FUTURE

Clive Dytor, the School's 150th Anniversary and beyond

"The sun sinks to rise again"
– Cardinal Newman: The Second Spring

The Oratory had a decorated Falklands War veteran to lead it into the 21st century. As a Lieutenant with 45 Commando Royal Marines, Clive Dytor broke the deadlock in an important battle for the craggy Two Sisters mountain. Under heavy fire he led the charge to take a heavily fortified Argentine machine gun position that turned the tide in the assault. For this action he was awarded the Military Cross. Indeed, Clive Dytor had led an interesting life. Educated at Christ College, Brecon, he then read Arabic at Trinity College, Cambridge. After

Opposite: The scene in Westminster Cathedral for the 150th Anniversary Mass on 2nd May 2009.

Right: Rt Rev. Monsignor Antony Conlon, Chaplain to The Oratory School and the Oratory Preparatory School.

leaving the Royal Marines he decided to seek ordination in the Church of England, studying at Wycliffe Hall in Oxford. He served, after ordination, in a parish in Walsall and then moved on to become Assistant Chaplain at Tonbridge School. At this point, his reading of the works of Cardinal Newman led him to turn towards the Catholic Church. Becoming a Catholic meant that he could no longer keep his position at Tonbridge School and he moved to St Edward's School, Oxford, as housemaster. It was while he was looking for somewhere to attend Mass in that city that he came across the Oxford Oratory where he learned that Newman had founded a school. He determined to become its Head Master. It seemed to him the next move in his unfolding life story. So he came to the interviewing panel for the headmastership with a great range of experience, an aptitude for leadership and an essential sympathy with the Founder's thinking.

Clive Dytor became Head Master in 2000, followed a year later by Alec Bradshaw as Bursar and Monsignor Antony Conlon as Chaplain. These three men were to become close friends and colleagues in a mission to lift the Oratory to the top rank of British schools.

Oratorians like Jamie Sehmer and Chris French. Mention must also be made in this context of the gentle and effective presiding role carried out by Michael Hasslacher, Chairman of the Governing Body and scion of a long supporting Oratory family. This development has been termed 'The Second Spring' – a reference to Newman's sermon delivered in 1852 in the chapel at Oscott at the First Synod of the assembled hierarchy which had been restored in 1850. Dytor and Alec Bradshaw had been drawn to the school through the life and writings of Newman, both having been parishioners of Oratory parishes at Oxford and Birmingham respectively.

The first building projects in 2001 were new History and Design Departments. Then St John and Faber Houses were gutted and refurbished. A planning application was submitted to clear a wood, and demolish buildings to make way for brand new FitzAlan and Norris Houses. South Oxfordshire District Council approved the application unanimously, and the O.S. was the base for an army of construction workers and their equipment over four years until 2006.

Above: The cricket field.

Top left: Lord Guthrie of Craigiebank opens the new Norris House in February 2008.

Left: Sir Clive Woodward opens the new building of FitzAlan House in April 2005.

On taking up his position in 2000 Clive Dytor's stated aim was to make the O.S.: "the best Catholic school in England". The Governing Body gave their strong backing to this endeavour and within the first year of the Millennium ambitious plans had been drawn up to upgrade the Woodcote site with new boarding houses and academic departments and a thorough renovation of the school itself. The Governors' Finance and Property Committees charted the way forward under the Chairmanship of Old

Top right: The Director of Music, Julian McNamara, rehearses the Schola Cantorum.

Top far right: Karl Hohenberg, Leader of the School Orchestra.

Above right: A performance of The Wizard of Oz by members of the Middle School.

Above far right: In the Tomlinson Arts Centre.

Right: Mrs Pauline Walker in the Housemother's room of St John House.

As the Houses were remodelled or rebuilt they were also being internally transformed by the introduction of the Dames (Housemothers). First Mrs Walker to St John and then all other Houses were given dedicated 'feminine influence'. The provision of a female influence on the boys had been a fundamental part of Newman's original vision for the School he shaped in Edgbaston and he had entrusted his friend, Mrs Frances Wootten, with that task. The re-introduction has been a resounding success proving the far-sightedness of Newman's educational thinking.

By the Summer of 2009 with new Art, English, Design and Technology, History, Mathematics and Theology Departments, the seven-year project had been completed. The Woodcote campus was augmented with the purchase of properties in Woodcote village. This, coupled with extra residential accommodation in the new Boarding Houses allowed Clive Dytor to attract academic staff of calibre from some of the leading public schools.

Sporting enthusiasm has always been strong at the The Oratory School. Now the School has started

producing Premiership Rugby players, England Youth squad cricketers, Great Britain rowers and shooters and, in addition, a professional footballer. Alongside the boys' physical life, Music and Drama have been reinforced, and the Advent Carol Service and Benediction have become highlights of the School's family year.

In 2007 the school was named the top Independent School for Sport by *The Daily Telegraph* and the following year *The Times* placed the O.S. in its top 30 Boys' Schools nationwide. The Art Faculty under the charismatic leadership of Paul Tomlinson gained national recognition as it was awarded Foundation status by the Examination Boards and then best in the UK for A Level, then GCSE Art and Design by the *Good Schools Guide*.

As the new buildings rose and the path for the School's future was laid out so it was the aim that the connection with the past should also be strengthened. Old Oratorians' Days on- and off-site brought together former school friends. In 2008 an Old Oratorian who had been both Cricket and School Captain during his time was appointed to the most senior legal post. Igor Judge became Baron Judge of Draycote and Lord Chief Justice of England and Wales. He also accepted an invitation to become President of the Oratory Association. He has written the Foreword to this volume.

The Old Chapel neglected over the years and gradually restored under Monsignor Vaughan Morgan's chaplaincy was impressively re-roofed and made into a place for quiet prayer and Daily Mass. It has been

Opposite: The Golf Course is popular with the boys.

Above: Rugby Football.

Right: Anthony Coupland holds his Bisley trophy (The Financial Times Cup).

Right: Sam Borg (School Captain) and Mat Anker (Captain of Boats) receive The Daily Telegraph Independent School for Sport Award, 2007.

Far right: Enthusiasm for cricket has always been a feature of the School.

153

Left: A service in the restored former School Chapel, now St Joseph's.

Below far left: Old Oratorian Captain Bertie Kerr meets up with fellow Oratorian Captain George Heyes (O.S. 1992–9) on service in Afghanistan, 2008.

Below left: Admiral John Lippiet, Inspecting Officer of the May 2008 Biennial Inspection, stands between Wing Commander Marland Green MBE (left), Lower Master and Commanding Officer of the CCF and Captain Bertie Kerr (O.S. 1997–2002) of the Royal Marines. To the right is Ronald Womersley, former CCF Commanding Officer.

re-named St Joseph's in recognition of Newman's great devotion to that Saint.

The names of significant figures from the past have been commemorated by the renaming of Old FitzAlan (Tomlinson) and Old Norris (Morey). With the new Houses and improved Faculty accommodation has come growth in numbers at the School not seen for two decades.

In its 150th year the School finds itself in excellent shape, almost completely rebuilt or refurbished, impressing prospective parents and hence attracting pupils. Preparatory schools which had never seen The Oratory School as the next option have begun to send parents to visit and regular visits by preparatory school heads aim to forge new contacts and spread the message of Newman's school further. It is significant that the

School's constituency has changed. The School's net is being cast more widely with visits to Old Oratorians and friends in mainland Europe. It now attracts pupils from a wider British and international community. The 2008 entry was a record.

Hovering over all this has been the prospect of the Beatification of its Founder. All this is seen as an auspicious sign that the Cardinal's spirit is still linked as closely as ever with his school. The stepping forward of boys with vocations to the Priesthood and conversions to the Catholic Faith from the boys, staff and parents have been witness to a deep movement at work in the School and also to the dedicated priestly ministry of

Above: The campus formed by the new buildings for FitzAlan House (left) and Norris House (right).

Right: Clive Dytor, Head Master, with Sam Borg.

Far right: Sixth Form Biology.

Below right: Pat Thomas, Housemaster of St Philip House, with some of his charges.

Below far right: Paul Tomlinson, Director of Art, instructs a student.

Below: The CCF on a Field Exercise.

Monsignor Conlon, always supporting and encouraging boys and staff in their daily lives.

This book's narrative has told the unfolding story of one of the two institutions founded by Cardinal Newman which survive to the present day. It is a story of the survival of an educational vision that has emerged successfully against the odds, which include three changes of location and two financial crises.

When Newman was made a Cardinal in 1879, he received a number of addresses of congratulation, to which he replied with heartfelt thanks. One such address was presented by the Oratory School Society, on behalf of the Old Boys. In Newman's reply to them he stated "Day schools are not schools except in school hours." In this statement he was expressing his belief that the School itself should form a family, a community surrounding its pupils, supporting and developing them to become balanced and thinking members of society.

Many people have tried to encapsulate the elusive ethos of Newman's school. By common consent it involves something of the following. The individual should be paramount in education. A school system should be there to help individual pupils discover their special gifts. Individuals are not there to feed the ambition

or the glory of the system, least of all to be instruments of social engineering. When individuals feel they are valued and appreciated then they will be less inclined to confront the educational structure and those running it as they will feel that their personal dignity is respected. Through inclusion and mutual respect, the delicate problem of convincing the adolescent to conform is on its way to being resolved. In this respect, as in so many others, Newman took his inspiration from St Philip Neri. The youth of Rome with all their questionings, uncertainties and rebelliousness found in St Philip someone whose understanding of their situation attracted them. If the young feel valued and are able to empathise with those in charge they will also be more ready to consider the moral compass that is offered to them.

Comments of those who have observed The Oratory at close quarter lend credence to this proposition. Peter Burr (Member of Staff 1975–2003), who had previously taught at Christ's Hospital, once described an Oratory boy as one who "will look you in the eye and tell you what he thinks – politely".

The ISC Summary Report on the 2001 Inspection by the Independent Schools Inspectorate was of the following opinion about the School: "There is a strong sense of community and the impression of self-confident, happy, courteous, caring, trustworthy,

responsible and well-behaved young men indicates the success of one of its main aims."

Father Richard Duffield, who taught R.E. briefly in the School, once saw a group of O.S. boys outside Westminster Cathedral and remarked, "I thought they looked like Oratory boys – well-behaved but uncowed".

If all this is a valid description of that elusive ethos then The Oratory has much to teach the outside world. Perhaps that is where its future purpose lies now that it has reached stability and presentability.

If the above is convincing as an attempt to summarise the essence of the school that Cardinal Newman founded in 1859 and later, in conjunction with Ambrose St John

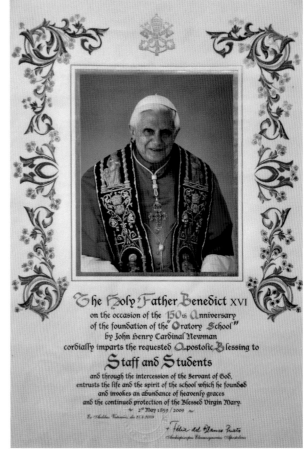

and John Norris, went on to mould, then there is a twofold miracle associated with its continuation. Firstly, that in spite of its many ups and downs, its spirit should survive recognisably for those who have known and learned to love it. Secondly, that this outlook should have become so ingrained in the School's concept of itself that it has been able to resist automatically all attempts, however well-meaning, however forceful, to make it change its sense of purpose. Many are the good people, Chaplains, Head Masters, Bursars, Teachers, Governors, who have aimed, for the best of motives to force it into a different mould

Right: The Papal Blessing received from Pope Benedict XVI for the 150th Anniversary of the School.

Below: Senior boys in various School colour blazers, ranging from (l–r) cricket, rugby, rowing and (on the right) to the distinctive design of the award for cultural excellence.

and have withdrawn unsuccessful in the attempt. In addition to this it has always managed to find the key person at the crucial moment for the solution of the immediate challenge.

On the 150th Anniversary of its Foundation The Oratory School is probably more robust than at any time in its long history: confident without arrogance, proud without pretence. The personality of Cardinal Newman still informs and the spirituality of St Philip runs like *'un fil di seta'* through the boys and staff. The School remains faithful to its Founder's vision, strong in its own identity and confident in its future in an uncertain world, cherishing the spirit of the Cardinal's motto at its centre:

'Cor ad Cor Loquitur' (Heart Speaks to Heart)

With the approval by the Vatican of the miracle submitted in support of Newman's Beatification (see back cover), the School's Founder is on course to become Blessed John Henry Newman, the ultimate goal being canonisation.

GOVERNORS, STAFF AND PUPILS

150th Anniversary, May 2009

President of the Association
The Right Hon. Lord Judge

Vice-Presidents
His Eminence William, Cardinal Baum
MFS Chapman TD MA DipEc
JJ Eyston MA FRICS KSG
The Most Rev Vincent Nichols PhL MA MEd STL

Governors
M H R Hasslacher Chairman
C J Sehmer FCA Vice Chairman
BFH Bettesworth FRICS ACIArb; The V Revd R Byrne BD AKC Cong Orat;
Mrs M Cochrane; Professor P W Evans MA PhD; F J Fitzherbert-
Brockholes MA; C J French; HH Judge KA Hornby BA; N R Purnell MA QC;
The Revd J N Saward MA MLitt; M W Stilwell; T A H Tyler OBE BA

Senior School Staff
C I Dytor MC, MA (Cantab) MA (Oxon) –
Head Master
Monsignor A Conlon – Chaplain
T J Hennessy, BSc – Acting Second Master,
    Mathematics, St John Housemaster
D Forster, MA MSc – Director of Studies

Academic Staff
Mrs E Aldington, AdvDip AD – Art
Mrs A M Blaseby, MA – Classics
S Bosher, BSc DipDes – Design and Technology;
    CCF
S A Bowles, BSc PhD – Chemistry
J A Brooke, BA, MA Head of GCSE – English
P W Brown, BSc – Physics
I A N Campbell, BSc – Physics
T N Danks, BSc, PhD – Head of Chemistry
D R Dixon, MBA – Head of Business Studies
P J Easton, BSc – Head of Biology
H A S M Exham, BSc – Biology
C W Fothergill, BA, MA(Ed) –
    Head of Classical Civilisation
G W Fox, ACP – Art
Mrs H R Fox, BA – Art

O P Garner, BA – French, Italian
O C Godfrey, BA – Head of Drama
M H Green, MBE, MEd – Lower Master, DT
Mrs S Green, BA – EFL, TEFL Curriculum Support
R Guillaud, Licence d'anglais – French, Spanish
Mrs K Hamilton-Bowker, Dip SpLD –
    Curriculum Support
M P Harrison, BA – Spanish, French
I Hart, BSc, PhD – Head of Science
Mrs F Harte, Dip SpLD, AMBDA –
    Head of Curriculum Support
A A Hill, MA, AIL – Head of Classics,
    Examinations Officer
Mrs N Jones, MSc – Mathematics
N J C Jones, BA, ARCO – Music, Asst
    Examinations Officer
S Jones, BA – Head of English
I P Jordan, BEd – PE, FitzAlan Housemaster
Mrs J M Kennedy, Dip SpLD – Curriculum Support
K Laughton, BA, AIL – Head of Modern Languages
G J Lyke, BSc – Mathematics
I C McLean, MA MSc – Chemistry
Mrs C Macnab, MA – Classics, Librarian
K E Macnab, MA – Religious Education
J P B McNamara, MA, FRCO – Director of Music

Mrs D A Nash, MA – Head of Religious
    Education, Head of Sixth Form and Careers
Mrs S M Nicholson, BA – English
R A O'Sullivan, BA – English
C N B Pohl, BA – Head of History, English
P E Poynter, BA – Head of Geography
Mrs D Redfern, BA – Curriculum Support
A N Stroker, BA, MA, PhD – English, Drama,
    Faber Housemaster
C J Sudding, BEng – Mathematics
C Sykes, MA MBA – Business Studies, Geography
Mrs E S Thomas, BA, MA(Ed) – French, Religious
    Education, Curriculum Support
P A Thomas, BA, MA(Ed) – Head of Economics
    and Business Studies, St Philip Housemaster
P L Tomlinson, MFA – Director of Art and Design,
    Senior Master
S C B Tomlinson, BSc – Director of Games, PE
N E Topham – CCF Admin Officer, Shooting
D O D Watkins, MSc – Geography, Philosphy
A J Wilson, MSc – PE and Games,
    Norris Housemaster
R B Womersley BEd – Ancient History, History,
    Geography
J M S Woodcock, MSc – Head of Mathematics

Senior School Assistants
D M Archibald
C J M Parlane

Sports Staff
M Eadle – Sports Centre Manager
T Huelin, BSc – Sports Centre Assistant
R Brown – Sports Centre Assistant
T Phipps – Sports Centre Assistant

Non Teaching Staff
A J Tinkel, MA – Archivist
Mrs L Coupland – Marketing and PR
D Chamarette – Media Consultant (p/t)

Registry
Mrs S A Waghorn – PA to the Head Master
Mrs E Henderson – School Secretary
Mrs M Lee – Secretary
Mrs G Munoz – Reception
Mrs J Martin – Reception

Medical Staff
Mrs P Codner, MSc RGN – Health Centre Sister
Mrs J E Tomlinson, SEN – Staff Nurse
Mrs M Naylor, RGN
Mrs S Hester, SRN, RSCN, HV Cert
Mrs M C Zelisko, BA, RGN, RSN

Bursary
A F Bradshaw, DMS, MCIM – Bursar and Clerk to
   the Governors
A Rajan – Acting Finance Manager
Mrs C Bleimschein – PA to the Bursar
C A Agg; Mrs M J Coley; Mrs H C Monks;
Mrs P Brown; R Asamoah.

Services Staff
M Sixsmith, BSc MPhil – Head of Computer
   Services
P Gudge, BSc MRICS – Estates Manager
Miss P L Cunningham – Domestic Services
   Manager

Miss L Grant – Assistant Catering Manager
G Parker – Head Chef
Mrs C Tyler – PA to the Services Department
Miss C Honey – Head of Grounds
H W Thorp – Clerk of Works
Mrs D W H Knox, BSc – Health and Safety Advisor

Housemothers
Mrs J Blount – Norris
Mrs D Fletcher – FitzAlan
Mrs J Harper – St Philip
Mrs J Hyde – Faber
Mrs P Walker – St John

Support Staff
Mrs L Murdoch – IT Support
C J Lawmon – ICT Technician
Mrs D A Green, CertEd – IT Administrator
Mrs M Arkinstall, BSc – Laboratory Technician
R P Hobbs – Laboratory Technician
Mrs S C Mainprize, BSc – Laboratory Technician

Prep School Staff
R J Hillier, MA PhD – Headmaster
Mrs C Gregory, MA(Ed) – Deputy Head,
   Head of Pre-Prep
A M S Willson, BA – Head of History,
   Director of Studies
C Sexon, BA UED BEd MSc – Senior Master
Mrs C Vaux, BA Cert Ed – Senior Mistress,
   Head of RE and PSE

Academic Staff
C Anderson, BA – Head of French
Mrs L Anderson, BEd LTCL
Mrs W Barrett, BA CertEd TESL
Mrs S Boccaccini, BSc
Ms K Butler, BSc,
Miss S Carter, BA(Ed)
Mrs S Cordillet, MA CAPES
Mrs H Cox, BMus – Head of Music
Miss A Crowley, BSc – Rosehill Housemistress
Mrs L Finch, BEd Dip HE – Years 3–4 Coordinator
Miss J Gould, BA
D J Holmes, BA – Boarding Housemaster,
   Head of ICT
Mrs A Hughes, BEd – Head of Girls' Games,
   Caversham Housemistress
Mrs H Hwang, BSc BEd
Mrs R James, CertEd Dip SpLD
Miss A Jenkins, Cert Ed Dip SpLD Cert TESOL –
   Head of Learning Support
Mrs C Kenton, BA HDE
Mrs A Kos, BA HDE
Mrs J Le Bars, BA CAPES

Mrs K Lewis-Holland – TEFL
Mrs A Mackenzie, NNEB RSH
M Mackenzie, BEd – Librarian
Mrs C Mackworth-Praed, BA(Ed) –
   Assistant Head of Pre-Prep
Mrs M Meikle, Dip SpEd
D Osborn, MA BPhil DPSE – Head of Mathematics
Mrs A Peters, Cert Ed
T Peters, BSc BEd – Head of Science
Mrs K Phillips, BA
Mrs E Reed, BMus
Mrs T Sexon, BA UED
P Smith, BA – Head of Classics,
   Branksome Housemaster
Mrs A Stanton, B(Ed) MBA
Mrs S Stewart, BA
P Towse, BA(Ed)
R Webber, MA
J E Williams, BSc – Head of Geography
Mrs M Williams, BEd
Mrs P Williamson, BA(Ed)
Mrs H Willson, BA – Head of Art and Design
   Technology
J Winch, BA – Head of English
C Winterbottom, BSc – Head of PE,
   Elston Housemaster

Teaching Assistants
Mrs M Antonian, BA
Mrs K Atkin
Mrs J Barefield
Mrs K Maitland
Mrs J Mason
Miss N Morteau, BA
Mrs S Nathanislsz
Mrs J Packham
Mrs A Stickland-Taylor, BA

Prep School Assistants
Miss J Drake
Miss A Hopkin
M Nuku

Registry
Mrs J Gaff, BA – Registrar/Headmaster's PA
Mrs E Hillier BA – Secretary
Mrs J Whittle – Secretary
Mrs S Bird – Administrative Assistant

Medical Staff
Mrs R McKenzie, RGN – Sister
Mrs J Campbell, CertEd – Senior Matron
Miss J Hazell – Assistant Matron
Mrs N Winch – Assistant Matron

Support Staff
L R Mackey – Services Manager
R Vincent – Catering Manager
Miss E Capel – Pool Manager
Mrs J Sutton – Laboratory Technician

Cardinal Newman's School

O.S. Roll

Surname	Initials	House	Year
Adesanya	O O	St John	L6
Ahman	S T	Norris	3
Albury	P D	Norris	5
Alker	R W A	Dean	2
Almark	J P	Faber	3
Altass-Gomez	C J G	St John	3
Amaechi	C A	Norris	4
Amaechi	F O N	St John	3
Anker	A D	Norris	L6
Annan	C C	St John	4
Ansell	N S H	Norris	L6
Archer	C J	Norris	U6
Arencibia	C	Faber	4
Armar	J N	FitzAlan	4
Arnold	J-C T	FitzAlan	L6
Atkinson	G C	Dean	2
Atkinson	T E	Norris	3
Au	H H H	Faber	3
Baker	C S	St John	3
Baker-Smith	B R	St John	U6
Ball	A C	FitzAlan	3
Ball	M C	Norris	4
Ballsdon	O C R	Norris	3
Banbury	J G	Faber	3
Barclay	J P F	Faber	3
Barden	D R D	Faber	3
Barker	T R	Faber	U6
Barribal	G M D	Dean	1
Bartkowiak	M A	FitzAlan	4
Bartlett	T W	Norris	3
Barwick	W P	St John	U6
Batty	N J	St John	L6
Beale	A G	FitzAlan	U6
Beale	J W	FitzAlan	5
Beck	S E B	Faber	3
Bell	J W	Pereira	1
Bell	S O	Faber	L6
Belo	O	Faber	U6
Bevan	C M	Norris	L6
Beveridge	G A	FitzAlan	4
Beveridge	L R	FitzAlan	U6
Bilinski	K	Norris	4
Bishnoi	A S	Faber	L6
Bishnoi	A S	Faber	L6
Bitirim	T S	FitzAlan	3
Bitirim	T	Pereira	1
Blake	C J	Dean	2
Blake	W B	FitzAlan	5
Boulter	K N	St John	4
Bowie	H R C	Dean	1
Bradshaw	C S M	Norris	L6
Bradshaw	J F T	Norris	4
Brazil	W H A	Norris	4
Brice	R T	Faber	5
Brimacombe	T J E	St John	L6
Britt	L D	FitzAlan	U6
Brock	E E	Norris	U6
Browne	C	Faber	L6
Browne	P R	Dean	1
Bruce	J	FitzAlan	3
Buiatti	S	Faber	4
Burgess	C A T	FitzAlan	3
Burgess	H R G	Pereira	1
Burr	W F	Norris	5
Bush	H R	Faber	3
Butler	H F	St John	5
Butt	O W	St John	3
Byrne-Hansen	C E	St John	U6
Cai	D	St John	L6
Campbell	E R	FitzAlan	U6
Campbell	M L	FitzAlan	4
Cannon	S P	St John	3
Carr-Jones	H O X	St John	3
Chan	C K J	Norris	U6
Chan	H C K	Faber	5
Chan	M K	Faber	3
Chandler	O R W	Faber	3
Chaplin	J A	St John	L6
Chbat	S A	FitzAlan	3
Cheer	T A	Dean	2
Chen	D	Pereira	2
Cheng	K O	Faber	3
Claoue de Gohr	P M L	FitzAlan	U6
Cleghorn	F R	Faber	5
Clifton	A J	Dean	1
Connolly-Graham	J P	Norris	3
Cope	H J	Norris	3
Corich-van der Bas	M R	Norris	5
Coupland	A W	Norris	L6
Croisdale	J A	Dean	1
Cumming	C A	FitzAlan	4
Cunningham	J D	Faber	L6
Dash	R F	Norris	L6
Davie	W M	FitzAlan	L6
Davies	T R	Dean	1
De Stefano	F P L	St John	U6
de Verteuil	C I	Norris	5
Dean	A M	St John	5
Dean	A	St John	U6
Deane	B G A	St John	4
Decesare	S	Faber	U6
Del Conde	C	Dean	2
Dempsey	J C	Norris	4
Dempsey	S C R	FitzAlan	U6
Dentamaro	L	Pereira	1
Dentamaro	L	St John	3
Depaauw-Holt	L R	Dean	1
Doe	J R F	Faber	4
Doe	W C H	Faber	U6
Duncan	D B	Faber	4
Duncan	J T	St John	4
Duncan	N M	Norris	5
Duncan	R K	FitzAlan	4
Dunn	C E B	FitzAlan	3
Dziewulski	J G L	Norris	5
Eadle	Z E	Norris	3
Edwards	T A E	Norris	L6
Eggar	T S	Faber	4
Ehimuan	E	St John	5
Ejikeme	E U	Faber	3
Engbers	H T	FitzAlan	4
Etheridge	C	St John	3
Evans	J R G	Dean	2
Evans	M P G	St John	L6
Ezeaka	K	St John	U6
Fenn	M B	St John	L6
Fernandez Garciarce	E	FitzAlan	3
Firminger	S E	Faber	5
Fitzgerald	T K J	FitzAlan	3
Fleming	J P B	FitzAlan	4
Folley	D C	St John	3
Folley	T C	St John	5
Forbes-Gearey	B R	Pereira	2
Fothergill	N M	Norris	5
Fowler	J D	Norris	2
Frank	A C	Faber	3
Freiherr von Mentzingen	J A N K M	Faber	3
Frost	L W	Faber	3
Frost	S P	Faber	5
Fu	W-Y	Faber	L6

Surname	Initials	House	Year	Surname	Initials	House	Year	Surname	Initials	House	Year
Gadsden Ricaud	P	Faber	3	Howell	G T G	FitzAlan	U6	Littlefair	B S	Pereira	2
Gallienne-Schmidt	C	Norris	U6	Hudson	T C	FitzAlan	3	Littlefair	E L	Faber	U6
				Huggins	J J	Faber	3	Lo	E C Y	St John	U6
Galvez	J A	St John	3	Hunt	T S	St John	5	Lockhart	G H	FitzAlan	3
Garamendi	I	Norris	4	Hurn	A J	St John	L6	Lockhart	O T	FitzAlan	5
Garciarce Davila	M	Dean	1	Hurn	J S	Norris	4	Macauley	N A	Norris	3
Gemmingen-Hornberg	J	FitzAlan	5	Huysinga	R F	FitzAlan	3	Macdonald	C J R	FitzAlan	5
				Huysinga	T J	FitzAlan	L6	Maitland-Walker	J M F	FitzAlan	3
Getty	J L	FitzAlan	U6	Ibru	O M O	St John	5	Maltese	M J G	Dean	2
Gibbs	R J	FitzAlan	4	Idelson	M V	FitzAlan	3	Maple	J A P	St John	3
Goddard	E J	Dean	2	Jackson	J	St John	L6	Marples	O E	Norris	5
Gonzalez	A	Norris	3	Jacobsen	C E	St John	3	Martin	C F R	Norris	3
Gonzalez Noriega	J P	Pereira	2	Jamieson	H M	St John	3	Mason	R A F	Norris	U6
Good	G P	St John	3	Jennings	B H	FitzAlan	L6	Mason	R W	Pereira	1
Gordon	F H M	FitzAlan	3	Jeong	J-H	FitzAlan	L6	Mason	Z A E	St John	3
Gordon	M R J	Norris	L6	Jiggens	J J	Faber	U6	Mayne	J L	Norris	4
Grant	A D	Faber	5	Johnson	F W	FitzAlan	3	McCallum	C R	St John	U6
Grant	G D	Faber	U6	Johnston	A G	St John	5	McCarthy	J D	Pereira	1
Gray	C	Pereira	1	Jones	A E	Dean	1	McGeer	T Q	Faber	L6
Greenland	M J	St John	U6	Jones	C A	Norris	3	McKay	R J	FitzAlan	5
Greenland	N P	St John	5	Jones	S L	Faber	3	McWilliams-Gray	J V	Norris	5
Groehe	M C M	FitzAlan	3	Katzinski	O H	Norris	3	Mearns	M J R	Norris	3
Hacking	G A M	Dean	1	Keeble	D J	Norris	5	Measures	T A	FitzAlan	U6
Haimes	C D	FitzAlan	4	Keenan	M P	Pereira	2	Merritt	T S	FitzAlan	4
Halliday	L J M	FitzAlan	3	Keeshan	J L D	St John	U6	Mew	H T	Pereira	2
Halliday	T J R	FitzAlan	U6	Keogh	C P	FitzAlan	5	Miceli Demajo	L	St John	U6
Han	J-H	FitzAlan	L6	Kilgallon	J W	Norris	4	Mills	E	St John	L6
Hare	O J	Pereira	2	Kimura	Y	FitzAlan	L6	Minien	J A	Dean	2
Harmer	A J	St John	3	Knight	R C G	St John	5	Mitchell	B J	FitzAlan	L6
Harris	T J	Norris	3	Knott	A J	Faber	3	Monro	K A H	Norris	3
Hartwright	E C	Pereira	1	Kobayashi	R	Norris	5	Montgomery	C D J	FitzAlan	3
Hayes	A C P	Norris	L6	Kocak	M M	FitzAlan	5	Morley	A V	Dean	1
Hayes	S G P	FitzAlan	4	Kopec	C A	Faber	L6	Morley	H J	St John	U6
Henderson	B J S	FitzAlan	5	Kwan	C H H	FitzAlan	5	Morrell	B T	Faber	5
Heslop	M J	FitzAlan	3	Ladanyi	S	Faber	4	Morrell	P D	Faber	5
Heywood	C A J	St John	4	Lale	G L R	Pereira	2	Moulder	J C	Faber	3
Hilton	J A	Faber	U6	Lang	R B	Faber	4	Moyse	R A	Norris	L6
Hiscox	E M	Norris	3	Langguth	N K O	FitzAlan	3	Muller	L	Norris	L6
Hiscox	T A	Norris	L6	Lau	H N K	FitzAlan	L6	Munoz Navarro	C	Pereira	2
Hohenberg	K	Faber	U6	Le Roy	G W	Dean	1	Nelms	R B	FitzAlan	L6
Holliday	O N T R	Norris	4	Le Roy	H E	FitzAlan	4	Newnham	J E	St John	U6
Hollin	J J	Norris	4	Lee	A G W	FitzAlan	4	Ng	H Y H	Pereira	1
Hollin	W R	Dean	2	Lee	D D H	Pereira	2	Norman	M	Dean	1
Holliss	C J	St John	U6	Lee	L P A	St John	5	Nugent	T M	FitzAlan	4
Holliss	J E	Norris	4	Lees	R E	St John	U6	Nwabuoku	K O	Norris	3
Holmes	T J D	St John	L6	Lennon	A W	FitzAlan	3	Nylander	A	Dean	2
Horn	C T	Faber	3	Li	C K	St John	5	O'Brien	C J	Faber	U6
Horne	B J	FitzAlan	L6	Ling	C H	Norris	L6	O'Brien	G B	Faber	U6

Surname	Initials	House	Form
Ogilo	B E K	FitzAlan	3
Ogu	E O	St John	U6
Olopade	A O O	FitzAlan	L6
Olopade	A O A	FitzAlan	3
Olszowski	R T	Norris	U6
O'Nolan	C	FitzAlan	5
O'Nolan	J	FitzAlan	U6
O'Sullivan	F J	St John	L6
Owen	J P W	FitzAlan	5
Packham	E R	Norris	L6
Packham	H J	FitzAlan	4
Palmer	L M W	FitzAlan	5
Pardo Posadas	P J	St John	4
Parker	C J	Pereira	2
Parry	A L	Dean	1
Patel	R	FitzAlan	3
Paterson	H G	Norris	U6
Payne	F W	Faber	L6
Payne	R C	Faber	4
Peggram	G A	FitzAlan	U6
Peggram	H A	Pereira	1
Perera Cabrera	R	Dean	2
Perez	L	Norris	4
Perryment	H O	St John	U6
Phipps	M T	Faber	U6
Polkinghorne	N J	FitzAlan	U6
Pollock	O W A	Dean	2
Poston	M G	Pereira	2
Proctor	F	St John	5
Quartey-Ngwube	O N-L	Faber	3
Quesada Reynoso	A	Norris	L6
Radley	J I	Faber	U6
Radnedge	C V	Norris	4
Radnedge	J O	Norris	L6
Ravenhill	E C	FitzAlan	3
Redfern	C J	FitzAlan	5
Reford	B P H	St John	5
Reguero Galisteo	A	St John	3
Richmond	O T	Norris	L6
Roberts	B A S	FitzAlan	4
Robinson	A M C	Norris	5
Robinson	A J	Dean	1
Rogerson	L A C	St John	U6
Rogerson	S J	St John	5
Rohla	R N W M C	Norris	5
Rosser	O F	Faber	5
Rostron	G W	Pereira	1
Rowe	M J	Faber	L6
Rowell	E T	Faber	U6
Ryan	J O D	Dean	1
Ryding	E A P	Norris	3
Sado	S	FitzAlan	U6
Saint-Laurent Heidemann	A E M B	FitzAlan	5
Sampedro Menendez	I	Norris	4
Sassi	P H A	Norris	4
Sawar	S	Norris	3
Sayer	A M	St John	U6
Scicluna	L	Norris	4
Scully	D J	Norris	3
Sexon	A P	FitzAlan	4
Sherriff	W J C	Pereira	2
Sherston	J J	Faber	U6
Simonon	C J	St John	4
Skipwith	C M J	FitzAlan	4
Smillie	J D	Norris	3
Smith	M A S	Faber	5
Smith	R C B	Pereira	1
Smith	S G	Faber	4
Soludo	O T	Norris	4
Spencer-Fry	J D E	Norris	3
Stanford-Beale	J R C	St John	4
Stanley	T P P	Dean	1
Stevens	M P	St John	5
Stevenson	B S	Faber	5
Stewart	M I	St John	U6
Stewart	M J	Faber	3
Stocken	A M	Faber	L6
Stockings	T M	Faber	U6
Stoddart	T E	St John	3
Stroker	E A	St John	U6
Suthon	G E	Dean	2
Swan	O J	St John	4
Sweeney	O J E	FitzAlan	U6
Tam	C H H	Norris	U6
Teasdale	D J	St John	4
Thomas	B U	Pereira	2
Thurston	J R	FitzAlan	5
Tihngang	A M	FitzAlan	L6
Trainer	M C	FitzAlan	3
Tritton-Price	G	FitzAlan	3
Tsang	H S L	Norris	4
Tsang	K Y C	St John	5
Tully	R	Norris	U6
Tully	S J	Norris	5
Turner	B W	Norris	3
Turner	R M	Norris	L6
van der Lande	E M B	FitzAlan	U6
van der Lande	G F P	FitzAlan	5
van der Pant	C L	Dean	2
von Bertrab	D	St John	4
von und zu Liechtenstein	J W K E B M	Faber	4
Walsh	C J	Dean	1
Wang	Z	Faber	U6
Ward	W J	FitzAlan	5
Warren	F J	Norris	3
Watkins	M J	St John	4
Wayne	D P V	Norris	4
Webster	T J L	Pereira	1
Welch	A J	FitzAlan	5
White	A J	Pereira	1
White	T J A	FitzAlan	3
White	Z	Norris	3
Whittaker	C G M	FitzAlan	L6
Williams	B A N	Norris	U6
Williams	D W	Pereira	1
Williams	J R	FitzAlan	4
Willis	A E	Faber	L6
Willson	W T	St John	5
Wilson	J A	Norris	4
Winney	M S	Norris	5
Winterson	M	Pereira	2
Wirth	N G	Norris	5
Wolf	O H	Faber	5
Wood	J C	Faber	5
Woodeson	G C H	Norris	U6
Woodward	F W	Faber	3
Woodward	W J	Faber	4
Wormald	M C	FitzAlan	3
Wright	W C L	Norris	3
Xie	J L	Norris	5
Yaxley	S C	Pereira	1
Ye	Z Y	Faber	U6
Zeng	X-T T	Faber	4
Zielinski	L G	Faber	4
Zielinski	M	Faber	L6

O.P.S. Roll

Surname	Year						
Alani, M.	5	Butler-Creagh, B.	R2	Edwards, M.	5	Hart, L.	6
Amaechi, L.	7	Butler-Creagh, E.	1	Egboga, C.	R2	Hart, M.	3
Anderson-Jeffs, A.	2	Campbell, M.	3	Egboga, O.	4	Hart, M.	8
Anderson-Jeffs, C.	7	Campbell, P.	2	Egboga, S.	6	Hart, R.	R2
Anderson-Jeffs, D.	5	Chandler, I.	6	Elkes, G.	1	Hart, T.	2
Antonian, E.	8	Christie, O.	4	Elkes, K.	4	Hatton, B.	5
Antonian, H.	5	Christie, S.	3	Elkes, W.	5	Hatton, Y.	4
Appleton, J.	6	Clark, H.	8	Elkington, K.	2	Hawkey, S.	6
Appleyard, F.	3	Cockings, A.	R1	Elkington, S.	4	Hayward, T.	1
Arkinstall, E.	6	Cockings, C.	2	Elliott, J.	2	Hearnden, A.	3
Armstrong, H.	4	Cockings, O.	3	Elliott, R.	1	Hearnden, O.	8
Ashley-Carter, C.	4	Coffield, S.	R1	Engbers, G.	4	Heath, P.	2
Ashley-Carter, J.	6	Colquhoun-Flannery, H.	6	Evans, G.	4	Henderson, J.	7
Austin, H.	3	Conboy, E.	4	Evans, R.	6	Hindley, G.	2
Baker, M.	5	Conboy, J.	3	Eyston, G.	1	Hindley, J.	2
Barker, F.	3	Cooper, J.	4	Farlow, I.	3	Hiscox, A.	6
Barker, T.	2	Cooper, Z.	R2	Farlow, S.	5	Hiscox, H.	R2
Bartolomei, A.	8	Cope, E.	5	Fernandez de Pinedo, B.	3	Hogan, A.	3
Baty, A.	8	Coppen-Manns, R.	6	Fernandez de Pinedo, D.	6	Hogan, S.	8
Bavage, A.	7	Cordell, D.	8	Fernandez de Pinedo, L.	4	Hogan, T.	4
Baxter, A.	2	Cormack, R.	7	Fernandez de Pinedo, N.	R2	Hogg, P.	R1
Baxter, M.	4	Cormack, R.	5	Fielding, C.	2	Hopkins, B.	8
Baxter, R.	6	Crowe, J.	8	Forbes-Gearey, T.	6	Horridge, O.	7
Bermingham, A.	2	Cummings, C.	6	Garcia Lamuno, J.	8	Houghton, B.	1
Bermingham, F.	5	Curry, A.	4	Garcia Lamuno, N.	6	Huysinga, L.	5
Bermingham, J.	6	Curry, O.	4	Gardner, N.	2	Hynes, R.	7
Bevan, W.	6	Cutler, T.	3	Gibbon, C.	4	Ingram, H.	3
Beveridge, C.	8	Daintree-Blackshaw, B.	R2	Goode, H.	7	Jackson, L.	2
Beyki, D.	5	Danks, B.	3	Goode, H.	5	James, C.	7
Bilinska, I.	6	Davies, H.	4	Gordon, C.	7	James, O.	4
Bindoff, E.	1	Davies, L.	R2	Gordon, F.	4	Jarvis, G.	R2
Bindoff, R.	R2	Davies, O.	7	Gordon, P.	6	Jones, A.	3
Bird, A.	5	Davies, S.	R1	Gowing, L.	6	Jones, B.	5
Birkholm, A.	5	de Gruijter, E.	8	Grant, D.	7	Jones, O.	6
Birkholm, P.	8	de la Macorra Mata, J.	8	Gray, J.	1	Jones, T.	6
Boccaccini, A.	R1	Dean, F.	5	Green, A.	6	Jordan, A.	5
Boccaccini, M.	R2	Deeny, C.	8	Green, K.	4	Jordan, C.	5
Bolton, M.	5	Deeny, L.	7	Green, R.	3	Jordan, H.	8
Bond, R.	5	Delicado, J.	6	Greenham, M.	3	Jordan, S.	7
Born, C.	R1	Dempsey, P.	7	Gregg, E.	1	Keeshan, J.	7
Born, E.	2	Derbyshire, H.	5	Gregg, H.	1	Kendall, L.	5
Braham, R.	7	Derbyshire, L.	4	Gregory, M.	5	Kendall, M.	7
Burnett, A.	R2	Domecq Serrano-Suner, P.	6	Griggs, Z.	3	Keogh, C.	3
Burnett, H.	5	Domecq-Martel, S.	6	Guerrero-Domecq, N.	6	Khan, J.	R2
Burrage, C.	1	Dowsett, E.	3	Haimes, G.	7	Khan, M.	3
Burrage, G.	8	Dowsett, I.	R1	Haimes, J.	3	Knight, J.	5
Burrows, A.	7	Dowsett, R.	1	Hamilton-Bowker, P.	4	Knott, A.	6
Butler, E.	2	Easton, A.	1	Harrison-Moore, A.	3	Knott, F.	1
Butler, P.	5	Easton, J.	4	Harrison-Moore, C.	R2	Lam, C.	8
		Easton, M.	R1	Hart, H.	7	Lamsdale, J.	R1

Langley, B.	5	Motha, M.	8	Rodick, A.	7	Thompson, B.	1
Langley, I.	4	Moyse, T.	8	Rodick, H.	3	Thompson, E.	7
Langley, L.	2	Newell, N.	2	Rohll, D.	4	Tipple, H.	7
Langley, M.	R2	Newell, N.	R2	Rosenfeld, E.	3	Tompkins, A.	4
Langley, R.	R2	Newton, G.	4	Rosenfeld, L.	2	Tompkins, L.	2
Leaver, A.	5	Newton, W.	6	Ross, E.	2	Tritton, E.	3
Leaver, C.	2	Nicoll, A.	2	Ross, O.	R1	Underwood, A.	R2
Leaver, G.	R1	Nicoll, J.	6	Rowe-Jones, A.	8	Underwood, M.	3
Lee, E.	4	Nugent, M.	2	Ryding, R.	6	Vidal de la Pena, M.	8
Lee, H.	1	Nugent, W.	1	Salmon, I.	2	Walker, J.	5
Leedham, A.	1	O'Brien, E.	2	Sandall, J.	8	Walmsley, A.	6
Legtmann, E.	3	O'Brien, W.	5	Sandall, J.	6	Walmsley, T.	4
Legtmann, I.	R1	Ogidi, J.	6	Sandall, R.	3	Warren, A.	2
Littlefair, G.	3	Ogilvy, B.	4	Seymour, A.	2	Warren, O.	5
Lockhart, J.	4	Ogilvy, M.	1	Sheikh, A.	8	Warren, P.	6
Lovett, A.	3	Ormerod, A.	1	Sheppard, C.	5	Watson, R.	1
Lovett, O.	6	Oxley, W.	4	Sheppard, R.	R2	Webb, G.	7
Lovett, W.	8	Packham, J.	8	Shiundu, V.	8	Webb, H.	5
Luchford, W.	7	Page, R.	4	Silverlock, A.	7	Webber, S.	R2
Lynskey, J.	R2	Painter, H.	1	Silverlock, A.	4	West, A.	R2
Lynskey, T.	2	Painter, M.	3	Soto, N.	7	West, G.	2
Mackay, M.	3	Parkes, A.	8	Southgate, T.	3	West, S.	4
Macnab, C.	7	Parkinson, T.	R2	Spears, A.	7	White, A.	5
Macnab, E.	8	Parton, T.	6	Spratley, J.	4	Whitfield, E.	7
Macnab, T.	6	Parton, W.	4	Sprules, R.	4	Whitfield, R.	5
Malcolm, A.	1	Pearce, C.	8	Stacey, W.	1	Wilder, G.	7
Maldonado, J.	6	Pearce, H.	6	Stafford, J.	1	Williams, A.	5
Marsan, T.	6	Perrott, T.	R1	Stanley, A.	6	Williams, E.	6
Martin, D.	R2	Powell, C.	6	Stanley, M.	1	Williams, J.	7
Martin, E.	2	Powell, W.	3	Stanton, C.	5	Williams, L.	R2
Mason, L.	4	Purkhardt, E.	5	Stanton, G.	2	Williams, S.	2
Mayer, A.	2	Purkhardt, T.	8	Stanton, H.	7	Willson, M.	7
Mayer, E.	R2	Radford, H.	4	Stanton, S.	1	Wilson, A.	8
Mayne, W.	7	Radford, J.	4	Stegeman, E.	5	Wilson, A.	R1
McAdden, F.	R2	Radford, T.	4	Stegeman, O.	3	Wilson, B.	6
McKenzie, N.	5	Ralston, A.	6	Stewart, J.	1	Wilson, B.	1
McKenzie, W.	8	Ralston, G.	2	Stone, H.	4	Wilson, J.	5
Merritt, B.	R2	Ravenhill, E.	7	Stow, G.	4	Wilson, O.	4
Merritt, D.	2	Reed, C.	4	Stow, J.	8	Winch, J.	4
Merritt, M.	7	Reed, J.	5	Stroker, L.	7	Winterbottom, J.	3
Mew, A.	1	Rees, I.	R1	Sturch, K.	6	Winterbottom, O.	R1
Mills, A.	6	Reynolds, D.	R1	Sudding, C.	5	Winterbottom, T.	1
Miron, J.	8	Richards, A.	6	Sudding, W.	4	Wisniewski, L.	6
Miron, N.	6	Richardson, A.	4	Sumeray, H.	8	Wisniewski, T.	8
Monger-Godfrey, T.	3	Richardson, J.	2	Surti, K.	1	Woodard, E.	5
Moran, M.	4	Richardson, O.	R2	Surti, R.	2	Woodard, J.	6
Moran, W.	1	Richardson, W.	3	Swanston, M.	4	Yates, C.	3
Morton, R.	5	Rintoul, C.	8	Szweda, J.	4	Yates, R.	7
Motha, A.	3	Rintoul, C.	5	Tchen, V.	8		
Motha, H.	5	Roberts, E.	8	Thomas, C.	2		

A SELECTION OF NOTABLE OLD ORATORIANS

Chapters 1 and 2 (1862–72)
Edward Bellasis (O.S. 1862–70) became Lancaster Herald and Registrar of the College of Arms and **Sir George Sherston Baker** (O.S. 1862–66) was an eminent County Court Judge and Recorder.

Chapter 3 (1872–1911)
In the Military: the brothers of Father Edward Pereira, **Brigadier-General George Pereira** (O.S. 1876–83) and **Major-General Sir Cecil Pereira** (O.S. 1880–88) were eminent soldiers, as were **Brigadier-General John Bell-Smyth** (O.S. 1879–85), **Lieutenant-Colonel Sir Martin Archer-Shee** (O.S. 1883–85), later the Conservative M.P. for Finsbury, **Lieutenant-Colonel Stephen Hungerford Pollen** (O.S. 1880–85) and **Lieutenant-General Sir Arthur McNamara** (O.S. 1890–96); **Lieutenant-General Sir Adrian Carton de Wiart** (O.S. 1891–98) is the only Old Oratorian to be awarded the Victoria Cross; **James Elmsley** (O.S. 1890–96) was a **Major-General** in the Canadian Army and commanded the British Expeditionary Force to Siberia; **Wilfrid Egerton** (O.S. 1889–) reached the rank of **Rear-Admiral** in the Royal Navy; **Rear-Admiral Robin Dalglish** (O.S. 1893–94) commanded the Australian Squadron and represented the Navy in international fencing matches as well as

being awarded a gold medal for 'Good Sportsmanship' in the 1924 Olympic Games; **Lieutenant-Colonel Edward Wickham** (O.S. 1901–08) served in the Indian Army and later became Conservative M.P. for Taunton; **Brigadier Humphrey Stronge** (O.S. 1902–06) was the U.K. Military Attaché in Prague at the time of the Munich Agreement; **Group Captain Joseph Smyth-Pigott** (O.S. 1903–05) served in the Royal Naval Air Service during World War I and was subsequently U.K. Air Attaché in a number of European embassies; **Major Rober Egerton** (O.S. 1902–06, 1906–11) was awarded the Military Cross in 1915 and later killed in the First World War and **Brigadier Guy Gough** (O.S. 1907–11) commanded the Royal Irish Fusiliers in the withdrawal to Dunkirk.

In Politics and Public Life: **Lord FitzAlan K.G.**, the 1st Viscount FitzAlan of Derwent (O.S. 1865–72), was appointed as the last Lord Lieutenant in Ireland; **John Boland** (O.S. 1881–90) was a leading figure in Irish Nationalist politics and, representing Ireland, won two tennis events in the 1896 Athens Olympic Games; **James Hope** (O.S. 1882–88), later 1st Lord Rankeillour, held ministerial office and was Deputy Speaker of the House of Commons; **Charles Mathew** (O.S. 1882–90) was, in 1921, the

first Old Boy to be elected to Parliament as a Labour Member; **Sir Francis Anderton** (O.S. 1871–77) was Chairman of the London County Council; **Philip Kerr** (O.S. 1892–1900) became the U.K. Ambassador in Washington D.C. in 1940; **Francis Blundell** (O.S. 1896–1900) piloted the Catholic Relief Act of 1926 through the House of Commons; the **Marquis du Parc-Locmaria** (O.S. 1906–10) was a Belgian diplomat and ended his career as Ambassador at the Court of Saint James and **Sir Theobald Mathew** (O.S. 1910–16) became Director of Public Prosecutions in 1944.

In the Church: **Father Hugh Pope** (O.S. 1877–88) joined the Dominican Order and was Prior of their house at Hawkesyard; **Father Denis Sheil** (O.S. 1875–84) was the last novice to enter the Birmingham Oratory in Newman's time; **Bishop Dudley Cary-Elwes** (O.S. 1877–81) was Bishop of Northampton; **Bishop Francis Vaughan** (O.S. 1888–93) became Bishop of Menevia; **Father Alfred Barry** (O.S. 1893–97) joined the Franciscans and became the Superior of Greyfriars in the University of Oxford and Definitor of the English Province; **Father Leo Ward** (O.S. 1908–12) became a missionary in Japan and **Father Richard Lynch** (O.S. 1901–09) joined the Oratory community in Birmingham and was Chaplain to the Oratory School Society.

In Academia: **Francis de Zulueta** (O.S. 1893–97) became Regius Professor of Civil Law and Fellow of All Souls College in the University of Oxford.

In the Arts: **Hilaire Belloc** (O.S. 1880–88) was an essayist, novelist, poet and travelwriter; **Wilfrid Rooke-Ley** (O.S. 1891–96) wrote for the *Radio Times* and became a broadcaster and **Arthur Power** (O.S. 1905–07), a friend and companion of James Joyce, was elected as an Honorary Member of the Royal Hibernian Academy

In Business and on the Turf: **Francis Norris** (O.S. 1893–95) was a key figure in the history of the Amsterdam Bank in The Netherlands; **Colonel the Honourable Richard Preston** (O.S. 1899–1901) was an important figure in mining and metals firms and **Sir Humphrey de Trafford** (O.S. 1906–10) was a Senior Steward of the Jockey Club and bred two classic winners, *Alcide* and *Parthia*.

Chapter 4 (1911–22)

In the Military: **Lieutenant-General Walter Lentaigne** (O.S. 1915–17) became an officer in the British Indian Army and Director of Military Operations in post-war India; **Neill Ogilvie-Forbes** (O.S. 1914–19) attained the rank of **Air Vice-Marshal** in the R.A.F.; **Brigadier John Crum** (O.S. 1915–20) became Military Attaché in Athens; **Brigadier Guy Prendergast** (O.S. 1919–23) was Second in Command of the Long Range Desert Group in North Africa during the Second World War; **Lieutenant-Colonel Francis Cave** (O.S. 1912–14) was in the Rifle Brigade and later had a vocation in the Church, holding the title Monsignor from 1961, and **Roland Walker** (O.S. 1911–18) rose to the rank of **Lieutenant-Colonel**, also taking holy orders on retirement.

In Business and Public Life: **Sir Philip Warter** (O.S. 1918–22) became President of the Associated British Picture Corporation and Chairman of Thames Television; **Paul Curran** (O.S. 1921–28) ran a successful family engineering business in Cardiff; **Alfred Hasslacher** (O.S. 1911–16) succeeded his father as Chairman of the family wine firm Deinhard and Company; **Ronald Symington** (O.S. 1914–18) and his twin brother **John Symington** (O.S. 1914–18) were partners in the port wine firm Messrs Dow and Warre and **Cuthbert Fitzherbert** (O.S. 1910–17) became Vice Chairman for Barclays Bank, as well as

Chairman of the Catholic Record Society. **Geoffrey Parmiter** (O.S. 1923–28) succeeded him as Chairman of the CRS and was also a prominent Tudor historian.

In the Church: **Father Stephen Dessain** (O.S. 1920–25) became a member of the Birmingham Oratory and was elected Provost.

In Public Life and the Law: **Sir William Teeling** (O.S. 1916–21) was Conservative M.P. for the Pavilion Division of Brighton; **Count Gatien du Parc-Locmaria** (O.S. 1913–16) served the Belgian royal household, becoming Gouverneur for the future King Baudouin; **John Gaunt** (O.S. 1919–23) settled in southern Africa and was elected as a Rhodesia Front Member; **Sir Richard Elwes** (O.S. 1914–20) became a High Court judge; **Richard Dean** (O.S. 1916–18, Governor 1934–49, Chairman 1949–77, President 1977–82) was a successful solicitor and a consistent supporter of the School in troubled times.

In the Arts and World of Ideas: Sir Richard Elwes's brother, **Simon Elwes** (O.S. 1915–19) was a portrait painter elected as a Royal Academician; **Kevin FitzGerald** (O.S. 1915–19) became a familiar name in the world of broadcasting and **Francis Turville-Petre** (O.S. 1914–20) became an archaeologist famous for the discovery of the Neanderthal 'Galilee Skull' in Palestine.

Chapter 5 (1922–31)

In the Military: **Major-General Charles Deedes** (O.S. 1927–30) and **Lieutenant-Colonel Conyers Scrope** (O.S. 1927–31) were both awarded the Military Cross during the Second World War; **Denis Gibson** (O.S. 1928–33) was an instructor at R.M.A. Sandhurst and retired from the Army as a Colonel; **Colonel Paul Dessain** (O.S. 1921–27) was awarded the Military Cross and was Military Attaché in Rome; **Colonel Freddie Hughes** (O.S. 1925–32) had a notable post-war career in military instruction and administration in South Africa, the Caribbean, the United States and Malaysia; **Colonel Archibald Noel** (O.S. 1924–31) also received the Military Cross during the Second World War and ended his career as Military Attaché in South Africa.

In Business: **Michael Chapman** (O.S. 1924–30) was Executive Director of Blue Circle Portland Cement; **John Posford** (O.S. 1926–32) was a marine engineer involved in the development of Felixstowe port; **Bryan Percy** (O.S. 1928–34) served with the Steel Brothers group in the Far East and

Count Jan Lewenhaupt (O.S. 1929–34) developed a successful sports goods business in California.

In Public Life: **Ray Hamel-Smith** (O.S. 1930–34) was Mayor of Port of Spain in Trinidad and involved in the foundation of British West Indies Airlines; **Sir Peter Hope** (O.S. 1925–) became Ambassador to Mexico; **Geoffrey Hitchcock** (O.S. 1929–34) was a member of the British Council who became Cultural Counsellor in the British Embassy, Paris.

In the Arts: **Steven Sykes** (O.S. 1927–33) became a well-known artist remembered for his mosaic of the Angel of Agony in Coventry Cathedral and **Adrian Brookholding-Jones** (O.S. 1926–31) served in the Ancient Monuments Section of the Office of Works and later advised the Historic Buildings Council.

In the Church: **Ernest Menken** (O.S. 1926–30) was a monk of Belmont Abbey, Herefordshire who later became Head Master of the Abbey school.

Chapter 6 (1931–38)

In Public Life and the Law: **Sir James Comyn** (O.S. 1933–38) was a leading barrister of his era and acted as Counsel for the satirical magazine *Private Eye*; **David Sykes** (O.S. 1933–38) as an internationally respected aviation expert; **David Lloyd** (O.S. 1929–35), had an impressive record of legal service in Warwickshire and **Michael Fitzherbert-Brockholes** (O.S. 1933–38) served for a time as Chairman of Lancashire County's Education Committee.

In Academia: **Christopher Tolkien** (O.S. 1937–41) became an Oxford don and the literary executor for his father, J.R.R. Tolkien.

In the Military: **Michael Stilwell** (O.S. 1933–39) was awarded the Military Cross during the Second World War; **Michael Tolkien** (O.S. 1934–39) was awarded the George Medal during the Second World War and **Denis Wellesley**, fifth Earl Cowley (O.S. 1937–38), was awarded the British Empire Medal while serving in the R.A.F.

In the Church: **Father Oswald Charleton** (O.S. 1930–35) became a priest of the Southwark Archdiocese; **Dom Hildebrand Flint** (O.S. 1935–39) became a monk of Prinknash Abbey, Gloucestershire; **Father Desmond Swan** (O.S. 1935–40) was ordained for the Archdiocese of Westminster and **Father John Tolkien** was ordained for the Archdiocese of Birmingham.

Chapter 7 (1938–42)
In the Arts: **Sir Michael Levey** (O.S. 1941–45) became Slade Professor of Fine Art at both Cambridge and Oxford and later Director of the National Gallery and **Jack Wiener** (O.S. 1940–42) became a film producer in the United States.

In Public Life: **Robin Allott** (O.S. 1939–42) served as Under-Secretary in the Departments of Industry and Trade.

In the Military: **David Wilson** (O.S. 1939–42) passed the Special Entry examination into the Royal Navy and was awarded the King's Prize on passing out of the Royal Naval College.

Chapter 8 (1943–53)
In the Military: **John Spiteri** (O.S. 1944–49) was Commander of the Armed Forces of Malta and **Anthony Wilson** (O.S. 1940–44) served with distinction in the Korean War.

In the Church: **Monsignor Vaughan Morgan** (O.S. 1947–49, Chaplain to the O.S. 1984–97) became the Principal Catholic Chaplain and Vicar General for the Royal Navy and took on the post of Chaplain of the School in his retirement.

In Public Life and the Professions: **Christopher Hurford** (O.S. 1945–49) entered politics in Australia where he became a Cabinet Minister and Australian Consul-General in New York, his services to Australia being acknowledged by his nomination as an Officer of the Order of Australia; **David Purnell** (O.S. 1949–50) became Lord Mayor of the City of Cardiff; **Paul Purnell** (O.S. 1950–53) entered the Law and became a Q.C. and **John Symons** (O.S. 1952–56) became a leading paediatrician.

In Business: **Ian Macdonald Hay** (O.S. 1949–53) became high up in the counsels of the Shell Petroleum Company; **Edward Thorneycroft** (O.S. 1941–44) combined a career in the Lloyd's insurance market with a lifetime's devoted service to his old School.

In Academia: **Dominic Baker-Smith** (O.S. 1950–55) gained fellowships at the University of Cambridge, followed by chairs in English Literature in Amsterdam and Cardiff.

Chapter 10 (1953–72)
In the Military: **Général Bertrand de la Presle, Honorary KBE** (O.S. 1954–55) has attained eminence in the French Army.

In the Law: **Igor Judge** (O.S. 1954–59) became Lord Chief Justice of England and Wales from October 2008; **Keith Hornby** (O.S. 1960–65) likewise became a judge and **Nicholas Purnell** (O.S. 1959–62) is a leading barrister, having taken silk.

In Academia: **Peter Evans** (O.S. 1959–64) has held chairs in Hispanic Studies at the University of Nottingham, and at Queen Mary and Westfield Colleges, University of London, and **Leonardo de Arrizabalaga y Prado** (O.S. 1961–63) held a Visiting Professorship at the Tsukuba University in Japan.

In the Arts: **Michael Berkeley** (O.S. 1961–66) is a composer and a broadcaster on musical matters; the **Bicât** brothers, **Tony** (O.S. 1958–63), as writer, and **Nicholas** (O.S. 1962–67), as composer, have produced material for both stage and television.

In Politics: **Edward Leigh** (O.S. 1963–65) is Conservative M.P. for Gainsborough and Chairman of the House of Commons Public Accounts Committee and **Jerry Hayes** (O.S. 1966–71) was Conservative M.P. for Harlow until 1997.

Chapter 11 (1972–2000)
In Public Life and the Professions: **Richard Cairns** (O.S. 1979–84) is Head Master of Brighton College; **Ed Conway** (O.S. 1993–98) is Economics Editor of *The Daily Telegraph*; **Paul Farmer** (O.S. 1979–84) is Chief Executive of MIND, the mental health charity; **Ben Pope** (1981–85) is a composer and conductor, whose work often features on television; **Adrian Bridge** (O.S. 1974–81) received the Sword of Honour at the R.M.A. Sandhurst in 1984 and **Ben Hughes** (O.S. 1983–88) also received the Sword of Honour in August 1992.

Chapter 12 (2000 – present day)
A number of Old Oratorians have made their mark, nationally and internationally, in the sporting activities which they practised while pupils in the School. These achievements contributed to the favourable impression made on the Judges for *The Daily Telegraph*'s Independent School for Sport Award in that newspaper's School Sport Matters Awards in 2007.

In Association Football: **Alex Pearce** (O.S. 2002–05) has played for Reading F.C. and in 2008 was called up for the Scotland Under 21 XI.

In Cricket: Danny **Housego** (O.S. 2002–07) was a member of the Middlesex Crusaders squad that won cricket's Twenty20Championship in 2008, **Benny Howell** (O.S. 200 1–07) has played for Hampshire and **Simon Steel** (O.S. 2001–03) has been a member of the Barbados Under 19XI.

In Real Tennis: **Christian Whittaker** (O.S. 2005–) has been British Under 18 Singles Handicap Tournament Champion.

In Rowing: **Mat Anker** (O.S. 2003–8) was a Junior British International, coming seventh in the coxless pair in the Beijing Regatta of 2007; **Tim Male** (O.S. 1988–94) rowed at lightweight level for Great Britain between 2001 and 2006, representing the country in the coxless four at the 2004 Athens Olympic Games; **Philip Poynter** (O.S. 1993–98) was a Junior British International in 1998 and **Max Richmond** (O.S. 2004–8) was a Junior British International, winning a Gold Medal in the eight in the 2008 Coupe de la Jeunesse.

In Rugby Football: **Mark Bruce** (O.S. 1996–2001) has represented Ireland in Sevens; **Danny Cipriani** (O.S. 1999–2001) has played for England; **Ayoola Erinle** (O.S. 1993–98) has played for England Saxons and Leicester Tigers; **Andy Vilk** (O.S. 1994–99) was appointed Captain of the England Sevens Squad for the World Sevens Series Tournament in Dubai and won a Silver Medal in the Sport in the Commonwealth Games.

In Shooting: **Anthony Coupland** (O.S. 2005–) was selected to shoot for Great Britain in the Cadet Rifle Team Tour to Jersey in 2009, after being Under 18 Champion Shot at Bisley the previous year; **Alex Davies** (O.S. 2000–7) was selected to represent Great Britain in the Athelings Team in Canada in 2007, where he won the Bronze Medal; **Nick Davies** (O.S. 2000–5) shot for the Under 25 Athelings Team and represented England in the European Long Range Match in 2008; **Henry Gilbert** (O.S. 2003–8) shot for the Great Britain Rifle Team in South Africa in 2009, having previously been a member of the U.K. Cadet Rifle Team in the Jersey Championships; **Chris Mitchell** (O.S. 2003–8) recorded a similar achievement, and **Mike Phipps** (O.S. 2002–) was another Oratorian invited to shoot with the U.K. Rifle Team in the Jersey Championships in 2008 and to join the Athelings Tour to Canada in 2009.

BIBLIOGRAPHY

The Letters & Diaries of John Henry Newman, edited by Stephen Dessain, published by Nelson, London, from 1965 onwards.

An Essay on the Development of Christian Doctrine, John Henry Newman.

A Contribution towards Oratory School Annals The Year 1858 by an Ordinary Member of The Oratory School Society, published 8 July 1887.

Newman Light in Winter, Meriol Trevor, Macmillan, London, 1962.

Memorials of Mr Serjeant Bellasis, 1800–1873, London, 1893.

The Idea of a University, John Henry Newman, edited by Frank M. Turner in the Series Rethinking the Western Tradition, Yale University Press, New Haven & London, 1996.

A Catholic Eton? Newman's Oratory School, Paul Shrimpton, Gracewing, 2005.

Newman's Idea of a School, Andrew Nash, The Oratory School Association, 1990.

The Oratory School Magazine, published since 1891 by The Oratory School Society.

Italian Journey, J.W. von Goethe, translated by W.H. Auden and E. Mayer.

Apostle of Rome A Life of St Philip Neri 1515–1595, Meriol Trevor, Macmillan, 1966.

Benedict XVI and Cardinal Newman, edited by Peter Jennings, Family Publications, Oxford, 2005.

Lord Acton, Roland Hill, Yale University Press, New Haven & London, 2000.

The Idea of the Oratory, Raleigh Addington of the Oratory, Burns & Oates, London, 1966.

Extracts from A School Boy's Diary, by a member of the O.S.S., London, 1887.

Further Extracts from A School Boy's Diary, by a member of the O.S.S., London, 1889.

Memoirs on the late Cardinal Newman and the Oratory School by Henri La Serre, formerly French Master at Edgbaston, Duke of Norfolk's Archives, Arundel Castle.

Gerard Manley Hopkins, A Very Private Life, Robert Bernard Martin, Harper Collins, London, 1991.

Coram Cardinali, Edward Bellasis, Longmans, Green and Co., London, 1917.

ISC (Independent Schools Council) Summary Report on Inspection by the Independent Schools Inspectorate, 28.10.2001 to 1.11.2001.

John Henry Newman, Ian Ker, OUP, 1988.

Newman and his Age, Sheridan Gilley, Darton, Longman & Todd (paperback), London, 2003.

Thoughts & Fancies, Lord Rankeillour, Nelson & Sons, London, 1939.

Apologia Pro Vita Sua, John Henry Newman, Penguin Classics, Harmondsworth, Middlesex, 1994.

The Catholic Schools of England and Wales, H.O. Evenett, Cambridge University Press, 1944.

Letters from Hilaire Belloc, selected and edited by Robert Speaight, Hollis & Carter, London, 1958.

Gervase Elwes, The Story of His Life, Winefride Elwes and Richard Elwes, Grayson & Grayson, London, 1935.

With O'Leary in the Grave, Kevin FitzGerald, Michael Russell, Salisbury, 1986.

O.S. Lives, Obituaries from The Oratory School Magazine 1962–1992, The Oratory School Society, Woodcote, 1999.

The Frenchs of French Park, Maurice French, Warminster, 1999.

English Roman Catholics and Higher Education, Vincent Alan McClelland, OUP, 1973.

Architectural Review (December 1928).

Beaumont v. Oratory, Ignotus, Robert Brodie & Son, Windsor, 1926.

My Father's Son, Richard Rumbold, Jonathan Cape, London, first published 1949, reissued 1958.

Out of Due Time – Wilfrid Ward and the Dublin Review, Dom Paschal Scotti, The Catholic University of America Press, Washington, D.C., 2006.

A Biographical Dictionary of Architects at Reading, compiled by Sidney M. Gold and published privately, Reading, 1999.

A History of the Popes 1830–1914, Owen Chadwick, OUP, Oxford, 1998.

Caversham Park and its Owners, John Malpas, published by the author, Caversham, 1997.

The Public Schools, Brian Gardner, Hamish Hamilton, London, 1973.

The Letters of Evelyn Waugh, edited by Mark Amory, Penguin Books, Harmondsworth, Middlesex, 1982.

Summing It Up, Memoirs of an Irishman at Law in England, James Comyn, The Round Hall Press, Dublin, 1991.

The Chapel is on Fire, Recollections of Growing Up, Michael Levey, Jonathan Cape, London, 2000.

The Devil Take the Hindmost, Denis Peto-Shepherd, The Pentland Press, Bishop Auckland, 1996.

Aeroplanes in my Briefcase, David Sykes, The Quiller Press, London, 1987.

Oxburgh Hall, The First 500 Years, The National Trust, 1987.

The Life and Death of Rochester Sneath, Humphry Berkeley, re-issued by Harriman House Publishing, London, 1993.

The Field,

The Papacy and The Modern State, F.R. Hoare, Burns Oates & Washbourne Limited, London, 1940.

Eight Decisive Books of Antiquity, F.R. Hoare, Sheed & Ward, London, 1952.

Europe and the Faith, H. Belloc, Constable and Company Limited, London, 1920.

The Original Order and Chapters of St John's Gospel, F.R. Hoare, Burns Oates & Washbourne, London, 1944.

The Oratorian, Newsletter of The Oratory School Society.

The Royal Engineers Journal, April 1994, Volume 108, No1.

The Life of Edward Bulwer, First Lord Lytton, the Earl of Lytton (his grandson), in two volumes, Macmillan and Co. Limited, London, 1913.

Touchstone for Tessa, Eric Walsh, published by the author, Perth, Western Australia, 2007.

The Second World War, Volume II, Winston S. Churchill, Cassell, London, 1949.

Tommy A Tribute, A.J. Cornwell, B.Litt., M.A., Honorary Obituarist, The Oratory School Society, The Oratory School, 1986.

Inspection of The Oratory School by the Independent Schools Inspectorate (ISI) 15th to 18th October 2007, Independent Schools Council (ISC), 2007.

Gilbert Foliot and his Letters, Adrian Morey and C.N.L. Brooke, Cambridge Studies in Medieval Life and Thought – New Series: Volume II, Cambridge University Press, 1965.

The Letters and Charters of Gilbert Foliot, an edition projected by the late Z.N. Brooke and completed by Dom Adrian Morey, Monk of Downside Abbey, Headmaster of the Oratory School, and C.N.L. Brooke, Cambridge University Press, 1967.

The Catholic Who's Who, 1952, London, Burns Oates, edited by Sir Harold Hood, Bt, T.D.

Roman Road, G.R. Lamb, London, Sheed and Ward, 1950.

Voruniversitäre Erziehung bei John Henry Newman, dargestellt am Beispiel der Oratory School (Pre-university Education in the Eyes of John Henry Newman, as Represented by the Example of the Oratory School), Doctoral Dissertation by W.G. Mohnen for the Rhineland Teachers' University, presented and examined on 2nd March, 1978.

The Birmingham Oratory Church, A History and Guide, Fr. Paul Chavasse of the Birmingham Oratory.

The Catholic Subjects of Elizabeth I, Adrian Morey, Rowman and Littlefield, Totowa, New Jersey, 1978.

Edgbaston, A History, Terry Slater, Phillimore, Chichester, 2002.

INDEX